Praise for *Magick For Pennies*

"A money attracting spell popular in the Middle Ages began "take a large emerald"; another reads "take seven golden rings". Sometimes modern magical advice seems equally unhelpful! But Catherine Kane's new book "Magick For Pennies" helps the modern seeker who wants to improve his money, or love, or health situation without a fairy godmother. This inexpensive book contains a huge variety of clear, step by step instructions for techniques that cost little or nothing but address all the usual hopes and desires. She tells you how to substitute, for example, brown paper for virgin parchment, how to make your own tools, and where to find bargains. Rather than rescuing the poor princess, she empowers the reader to take which affordable steps to change their own- to change YOUR own- life!"

Tchipakkan
Co-chair Changing Times- Changing Worlds conference
Metaphysical speaker, teacher and artist

"In this book, Catherine Kane has presented a chatty, informal overview of some of the more basic magical techniques. Beginners would do well by reading this, and there are plenty of goodies and hints for the more advanced practitioner."

Jane T. Sibley, Phd.
Traditional Norse practitioner
Teacher and speaker
Author of The Divine Thunderbolt: Missile of the Gods, The Hammer of the Smith, A Different Dragon, and Norse Mythology...According to Uncle Einar

"One can become very mesmerized by the idea of casting your line into the magickal pond of knowledge. Catherine Kane's book "Magick for Pennies" is a fantastic easy to follow guide to getting started. She talks to the reader and shares her insight like that really cool aunt you always wanted to talk with more. I hope that you listen to your intuition and pick up this book. "metaphysics gives the tools for getting more result that you like." and this book will help you learn how to use your magic to make the tools that you will need."

Rev. Freya Harris
Intuitive and Angel Communication
Founder of Spiritual Liberties Interfaith Ministry

"Magick For Pennies is a wonderfully down to earth metaphysical guidebook full of both the basic how-to of magical practice and practical tips for the frugal practitioner. A great combination of common sense advice, encouragement to trust your own intuition, and creative ways to make the most of what you've got. Beginners and experienced folk alike will find something useful in this book."

Morgan Daimler,
author of Fairy Witchcraft, Pagan Portals: The Morrigan, and By Land, Sea, and Sky

And also for Catherine's previous books

Manifesting Something Better

"The techniques in this book are invaluable. Who said wishes are for children? Catherine shows you how to use positive energy in a way that is simple, direct, as well as very effective. I have used many of these techniques myself with nothing short of wonderful results. So make a wish, simply ask for it. Wouldn't it be wonderful if everyone read this book and learned how to make their life happier, healthier, and just that much more Wonderful?"
-Alexis Doyle
Internet radio show host

The Practical Empath-
Surviving and Thriving as a Psychic Empath

"...Gives you a window of understanding as to who an empath is, a brief synopsis about energy and how it works, shielding techniques, how much input is too much, and so much more. Cathy is an amazing empath who has helped countless people to learn how to deal with this wonderful however sometimes daunting gift. This book makes a great read for the novice and the experienced empath alike. With Cathy's guidance, you will learn how to cope with being an empath and, hopefully, you will get as much, if not more, out of her book *The Practical Empath* as I did. Happy reading."
-Delilah Kieffer, spiritualist and psychic

The Psychic Power of Your Dreams

Once again Catherine Kane has created a wonderfully accessible experience, like a visit with your fairy godmother with cocoa and cookies, wrapped up in an easy to read book. Have you been wondering if your dreams have something important to tell you? and if they do, how do you figure it out?

People have been writing dream interpretation books since the time of the Pharaohs, in Greece, Rome, and the Middle Ages, ..right up to the present, because humans spend a third of their lives dreaming, and the centuries have proven the value of paying attention to dreams. What makes this book especially valuable is that she recognizes that all dreams are not the same and cannot be read the same way. She describes many sorts of dreams and how you can work with them. (If your nightmare is from indigestion, better lay off the spicy snacks before bed!) How to tell the difference between literal and symbolic psychic dreams, and how to decipher your own personal symbol set (because your dreams don't use someone elses'). So this is not a book where you can look up crocodile, and read "If a man sees himself in a dream eating crocodile flesh it is good omen, meaning he will become a village official." (Yes, that's one of the Egyptian ones.)

Going beyond that, Cathy gives you lots of helpful hints (as any good fairy godmother would), about how to remember your dreams better, how to program your dreams, how to get the messages your dreams are trying to send; in short, she has a bit of something for everyone, delivered in a relaxed, friendly manner, that will make exploring these new skills easy and fun.

-Tchipakkan

Co-chair Changing Times- Changing Worlds conference
Metaphysical speaker, teacher and artist

The Lands That Lie Between

This book is an urban fantasy, the story of a girl who leaves home with her cat, moves across country, and starts a new life. After getting a tarot reading her fresh start gets a twist though when magical things start to happen around her. At first Morgan dismisses the strange events, but soon she finds herself embroiled in an adventure - with her trusty cat by her side - to find a gateway into Fairy and help choose the new king before the bad guys get to her and take her out. Fast paced and fun, with like-able characters and touches of genuine mythology interwoven with the authors story, it's reminiscent of old fairy tales or quests. The book has a light tone, and although it does include some violence and adult themes it would be appropriate for younger readers, or for older readers looking for something light and enjoyable. I'm looking forward to more from this author and hope this turns into a series.
-Morgan Daimler,
  author of Fairy Witchcraft, Pagan Portals: The Morrigan, and By Land, Sea, and Sky

Adventures in Palmistry

"The information in this book is clear, concise, hits the pertinent points of palmistry, and immediately lets you start practicing your craft."
-Adam Latin, professional palmist

"Ms. Kane is not only a talented palm reader, but a talented writer as well. She explains the concepts and techniques clearly, and with a sense of humor."
-Lois Fitzpatrick, leader, East Kingdom Soothsayer's guild, which studies the methods and history of psychic readings

Magick For Pennies:

Affordable Metaphysics

For Everyone

By Catherine Kane

Also by Catherine Kane

Adventures in Palmistry

The Practical Empath-
Surviving and Thriving as a Psychic Empath

The Lands That Lie Between-
An Urban Fantasy with Morgan and Sam

Manifesting Something Better-
Easy, Quick and Fun Ways
To Manifest the Life Of Your Dreams

The Psychic Power of Your Dreams:
Practical Skills for Working With Your Dreams For
Insight, Information, Creativity and a Better Life

For more information, please visit Foresight Publications at
www.ForesightYourPsychic.com

Magick For Pennies:

Affordable Metaphysics For Everyone

By Catherine Kane

Magick For Pennies:
Affordable Metaphysics for Everyone©September2014
by Catherine Kane

ISBN 978-0-9846951-3-3

Foresight Publications
Wallingford, CT.

Dedication

To those who make the most of whatever they've got

To those whose dreams are bigger than their pockets

To those who start with little and manifest miracles

This book is dedicated

May you always find a way
to make your dreams come true

Catherine

Acknowledgments

Here we are- the sixth book. Who would'a thunk it? What a long, strange, and wonderful trip it's been. As always, it's my name on the cover, but there's a whole host of other people who have supported me in writing- and it's time to say thanks.

To my readers and reviewers- Jayee White Oak, Morgan Daimler, Jane Sibley, Tchipakkan, and Rev. Freya Harris. This book is better because of you.

To the leadership and members of the Fairfield County Writer's Group. Near or far, you guys keep me writing.

To every teacher or vendor of things metaphysical who goes above and beyond to share information and items that can make people's lives better. I've learned a lot from you and people like you.

My special thanks to Jane Sibley, Tchipakkan and Starwolf for their specialized information. I don't know everything but it's good to know people who do.

To those of you who read my books. If you've come here before- welcome back! If this is your first time- welcome onboard! Either way, let's travel together for awhile and try and make our unique journeys better one in the process.

And finally, a special extra thank you to my husband Starwolf. You love me as I am, writer-y stuff and all, and your love and support sets me free to create books that can help people. Thank you.

Table of Contents

Introduction

The world is full of wonder. The world is full of amazing things. The world is full of miracles. And the world is full of ways that we can make wonders and amazing things and miracles happen.

Welcome to the world of metaphysics, where intention and alternative health practices and energywork and magick let us shape the nature of the world around us.

Metaphysics can be amazing and useful and fun. The problem though is that it sometimes it seems like it can become very expensive. Books. Classes. Crystals. Gadgets and thingamabobs. There's always something new to buy, and a lot of those things aren't cheap.

Have no fear. Cathy's here; and this book is going to look at different ways that you can work with energy, focus and intent without emptying out your wallet in the process.

Metaphysics doesn't always have to be pricey. Magick and herbalism and energywork go back through the halls of history, and many of these different practices started out with common supplies that you could find around the house, or in nature, or hidden inside your own head and heart. That's still true today. There are lots of pretty tools and supplies that you can buy, but there are also lots of other less costly options.

Don't get me wrong here. I'm not saying that you shouldn't buy metaphysical books and tools if they speak to you. I love metaphysical shopping and have bought more than my share of really cool items to work and play with. I'm just saying that metaphysical shopping is a lot like grocery shopping. When you go to the supermarket, there are some items where the high-end, brand-name specific product will matter, and there are some items where you get the basic generic variety (because frozen carrots are frozen carrots, no matter whose name is stamped on the bag...)

I'm here to show you ways that you can save money while you explore metaphysics. Save because your budget is tight. Save because something that you made speaks to you more than something someone else made. Save so you can build up a fund to pay for a metaphysical class or tool you might not otherwise be able to afford.

So let's get started...

Chapter 1
Magick and Money and You

If you're reading this book, you're interested in magick and metaphysics. If you're reading this book, you're also interested in saving money and making the most of whatever resources you have to work with; and that's a good thing. Each and every one of us has our own path to follow and our own amount of resources to carry us along on our journey. At that point, making wise use of your resources will move you further in the direction of your dreams, no matter what they are.

There are lots of different types of metaphysics, and this book will not teach you how to do everything. If I tried to do that, I'd have a book that you couldn't lift, and the price of it would shoot sky-high. That's the opposite of what I'm trying to do here. I want to give you a workable resource to make magick affordable. This book is here to show you different ways to explore your own unique metaphysical journey without emptying out your bank account. How to get the most magick for your money.

To do this, we'll start with some basic metaphysical concepts (the ones that lie at the heart of most magickal practice.) We'll look at how frugality and shopping smart work, and at lots of ways of how this applies to magick. I'll give you plenty of examples of how to do/ acquire/ build/ create things affordably, so that you have a smorgasbord of ideas to choose from.

Then, once you've got your options, it's your turn to create your own personal metaphysical shopping plan; and, when you decide what types of metaphysics speak to you, to learn more about them from other sources.

This is not a "One Size Fits All" universe. What you need and want may be different from what I need and want. What you need and want now may be different from you need and want in the future. The point is to know how to use your resources wisely at any time of your life.

Keep in mind that your idea of inexpensive and affordable may differ from mine based on your unique needs and tastes. When I go grocery shopping, I may need the more expensive brownie mix, but be fine with the house brand potato chips. When I go metaphysical shopping, I may buy the bulk bag of basic tea lights but want the really snazzy candle cup.

You may have totally different tastes and priorities-and that's great. The bottom line is give you the tools to develop your own plan where you save where that works for you and spend where that matters to you; and to have a shopping plan that's your shopping plan, not someone else's idea of what your plan should be.

At the end of things, your life is your life. Your budget is your budget. Your plan is your plan. And your plan and your budget and your life will work best for you if you've chosen what's important to you.

So, let's make some magick and save some money while we do....

Part One

Metaphysical Basics

Chapter 2
The Building Blocks of Magick

You may be new to metaphysics. You may be an old hand, but looking to try new things, or to find ways to afford to expand your present practices. In either case, we're going to start with the basics of most metaphysics, so we're all on the same page here.

First, let's take a quick look at these important concepts:

- Energy,
- Intention,
- Focus,
- Attraction, and
- Ethics

Energy- In metaphysics, we believe the world is made completely of energy. When you think about it, that's not far from how science views it. Science says that, at the atomic level, everything's made up of tiny particles, held together or pushed apart by energetic fields.

In metaphysics, we believe that this energy can be shaped or altered by both physical and non-physical means, and that, by working with energy, you can affect the nature of reality around you.

You're always interacting with the energy around you and having an effect on it. Metaphysics just gives you tools for getting more results that you like, rather than random effects that you may like or you may not.

Intention- Intention is just a fancy term for a goal, and setting an intention is setting a goal. When you're going someplace, you're more likely to get there if you choose your destination before you set out, and when you're working with energy, you're more likely to get a result that you like if you start with your goal in mind, and keep it in mind as you go along.

Intentions can be set by thinking, by speaking them out loud, by writing them down, and in lots of other ways.

Focus- In general, what you give most of your attention, your time, your energy, and your resources to is what you tend to get most of in your life. That's true whether you focus more on things you want, or on things you don't. For that reason, it's good to keep track of what you're focusing on, and try to give as much of your time and energy as possible to focusing on the things you want to bring into your life, as opposed to getting distracted by or hung up on what's wrong or could go wrong.

So, if you want to work with energy, you first set your intention, and then you keep your focus on what you're trying to attract or create, rather than be distracted by the million other interesting or annoying things in the world around you. Pretty clear, that.

Attraction- The basic concept of attraction (also known as the Law of Attraction) is that everyone and everything has an energetic field, and that an energy field attracts things with similar energy fields and repels things with different energetic vibrations.

Your energy is currently attracting people, things, and experiences that are a match for it into your life. By understanding how this works, you can adjust your vibration to attract more of the kind of things you want.

- You set an intention.
- You focus on what you're trying to bring into your life.
- And your intention and focus come together to shape the energy around you and affect what is happening in your world.

One interesting part of this is that you don't just attract the thing that you're focusing on. You also attract other things that vibrate at a similar frequency. For instance, if I focus on chocolate chip cookies, I may not only attract more cookies, I may also attract more positive and friendly people (and if I focus a lot on a cranky co-worker, I may not only find that co-worker seeks me out more, but that my car suddenly breaks down.)

Each of these pairs may at first seem to have nothing in common, but truth be told, each paired item makes me feel similarly happy or miserable, and that has a direct affect on my personal energy field.

That's one reason why it's a good idea to stay as positive as you can at any moment. It makes you more likely to attract cookies and less to attract chaos.

Ethics- The final concept in this chapter is metaphysical ethics. At its simplest, this consists of one basic point:

when working with the nature of reality, don't mess with other people's lives.

People are all given Free Will, the ability to make choices (good, bad or indifferent) and, by making such choices, have a certain amount of control over the nature of their lives. Metaphysics is one tool that you can use to make such choices, and it's fair to use it for that; but it's not fair to use it to interfere with the Free Will of others or to harm them.

To give you some examples:

- Attract a job- fine. Take a job away from someone else- not good.
- Attract a romantic partner- fine. Attract a specific person- not fine. Break up a relationship so you can attract a specific person- not good.
- Wish to be protected from someone who's giving you problems- fine. Wish something terrible would happen to someone who's giving you problems- not good.

See how that works? Since there's plenty of good things in this universe and we're not all looking for the same things, it's perfectly fine to try to attract more good things into your life. Problems only arise when you interfere with someone else's free will or actively wish harm to someone.

There's a rule in metaphysics called the Rule of Three, which says that whatever you put out there, for good or ill, comes back to you threefold- and nobody wants bad energy coming back to them in threes. We should act ethically in metaphysics because it's the right thing to do, but it also has the pleasant side effect that it puts out only good energy to be returned with interest.

When you respect the free will of others and wish yourself well without wishing others ill, you live a good life and also get better results.

So, energy, intention, focus, attraction and ethics. There's the big five that we'll be working with in many different ways throughout this book. There's a lot more to these than we can cover here, but this gives you the basic concepts to start out with.

And now that you've got the basic building blocks of metaphysics, let's next take a look at how to deal with negative or unwanted energy.

Chapter 3
Clearing and Protection

You've now got the basics of metaphysics-concepts you'll use again and again. Let's follow that up with some basic skills- how to protect yourself and your space from energy you don't want, and how to clear unwanted energy from yourself and your tools and supplies.

The first thing that you need in metaphysics is good energetic shields. Good shields surround your energy field like a science fiction-type force field, keeping out things that could harm you.

Here's a simple way to start developing your shields. Whenever you have a moment, close your eyes and picture yourself surrounded by light. On your left and your right; in front and in back of you; over your head and under your feet; so you're surrounded completely by light.

What color of light? Tradition says it should be white, as the highest/purest/best color which contains all other colors. I say chose whatever color makes you feel safest/ calmest/ best. You can also have more than one color. Mine are white with a gold edge.

As you picture this light, set an intention to define what your shields will do for you.

- Intend that you're protected from any energy that could harm you in body, mind or spirit.
- Intend that no energy will directly touch you unless you consciously choose to let it.
- Intend that you're aware of energy surrounding you, but that it cannot affect you.

- Intend that your shields are always protecting you unless you consciously chose to let them down.

What would you like your shields to do?

Over time, as you picture your shields, you'll find you feel more protected and more able to cope with the energy that surrounds you. This gives you more control of your own personal energetic vibration.

You now have shields to help control what energy affects you. What if (as sometimes happens) negative energy gets by your shields (or what if your negative energy is a "do-it-yourself" project?) At that point, you need to know how to ground out energy you don't want.

Grounding out energy is releasing unwanted energy into the earth, usually with the intention that the earth will recycle it into something beneficial for all. There are lots of different ways to ground out energy. I'm just going to talk about one here- grounding out energy with water.

Symbolically, water is strong and powerful. It's fluid, flexible, and darn near unstoppable. (Ever try to fix a leak in your basement?).Water is useful for clearing energy you no longer wish to carry in you, whether your own energy or energy which has come from outside of you. You can use it to clear cranky or negative emotions, feeling overwhelmed after a crisis, outgrown or dysfunctional beliefs, excess energy, and much, much more...

At its simplest, ground out energy (outside energy or your own) by combining two things:

- water (real or visualized), and
- your intention for the water to carry away energy you do not want or no longer need.

14

For example:

- Shake hands with someone who feels untrustworthy (like they "slimed" you?) Wash your hands with the intention to clear any negative attachments.
- Challenging encounters with people this side of hysteria? Beginning to feel a little hysterical yourself? Climb into the shower and picture the water carrying the stress of the day away.
- Someone yelling at you at work? No immediate access to water? Close your eyes. Picture an energetic waterfall passing over and through you, clearing you of bad vibes.

You get the idea...

It's important when you do this to include in your intention the idea that all negative energy will be cleansed, recycled or otherwise transformed for the highest good of all concerned. Don't want no free-roaming negativity out and about...

Just remember- when it comes to grounding, water is your friend, so go with the flow...

You've protected your own energy- now how about your space? Warding is the magickal way of protecting the energy of a space by creating a permanent energetic barrier around it. It helps protect a place from unwanted energies and entities, and can also make that place far more comfortable for the energetically sensitive person.

First start out by cleansing the area you're going to ward. (It makes no sense to shut negative energy inside with you.) Combine a physical cleaning with an energetic cleansing, using salt & water, smudging with sage, sweet grass or rosemary, or smudging with sound. (See chapter 12 Working With Sound.)

The next step is to cast a circle. There are many ways to do this, depending on your particular metaphysical or spiritual path, but here's a basic guide to start with.

- Face east. Say "Spirits of East, Powers of Air, guard this circle and all within."
- Move clockwise to the south. Say "Spirits of South, Powers of Fire, guard this circle and all within."
- Move clockwise to the west. Say "Spirits of West, Powers of Water, guard this circle and all within."
- Move clockwise to the north. Say "Spirits of North, Powers of Earth, guard this circle and all within."
- Move back to the East. "Say the Circle is cast."

If you were casting a circle for a temporary situation, like a ceremony, you'd have candles at the four points of the compass. Since wards are a permanent circle, you use crystals instead. (The best ones for this are double terminated crystals). These act as "repeaters", keeping the circle up even if something physical crosses it. If you're outdoors, you can bury these. If you're indoors, mount them in a holder, such as a wooden candle cup.

(Note- If, for some reason, you need to take your circle or wards down, start in the north, saying "Spirit of North, Power of Earth, Go if you must, stay if you will yet if you go elsewhere, let none be harmed by your movement." Move counterclockwise to each of the other three points, repeating the release statement to water, fire and air in turn.

Finish by saying "The Circle is open.")

You've got shields and wards. You've grounded out negative energy. Now what about those tools and supplies you'll be bringing into the squeaky clean space? I'm not saying that things you buy or find are automatically contaminated, but, as one of my grandmothers used to say "You don't know where it's been." Things that have been in stores or warehouses or out in nature may have had contact with many people and other things. Each of these has the potential to leave a bit of energy behind- and not all of that energy is going to be what you want to be working with. Best to clean house and start fresh.

There are lots of different ways of clearing the energy of an item or material. You can let it sit in sunlight or moonlight for a day or a cycle. You can bury it in salt or in the ground for a time. You can hold it under running water. You can clear with intention alone. The method you choose depends both on your personal situation and on what you're clearing (Some stones are water soluble. Some herbs will decay if buried.) Regardless of the method you choose, the main thing is that you set an intention that the item will be cleared of all energy that will not work well with you and all not belonging to it.

Once cleared, your tools and supplies are ready to use.

Just as it's important to know the basics of how magick works, it's also important to know how to keep outside energy from interfering with you and what you're trying to accomplish. Shields, grounding, wards and knowing how to clear your tools and supplies gives you control of what energy will affect you and gives you a clean and clear space in which to work.

In the next chapter, let's look at start looking at various types of metaphysics and how to figure out what's the best for you.

Chapter 4
Finding Your Magick

We've gone over energy, intention, and focus; the basic building blocks in most metaphysical practices. We've talked about attraction and how energy and focus can draw things we want and things we don't want into our lives. We've looked at ethics, and how to do the right thing. We've touched on energetic protection and how to clear ourselves and our tools of negative energy.

At this point, especially if you're new to all of this, you may be asking yourself "So what kind of metaphysics should I be doing? Is there one that's better or one that's worse? Is there one that I shouldn't be going near at all?"

Well, just as you need a metaphysical budget that works for you, you also need a plan of metaphysical practices that works for you as well.

This is not a "one size fits all" Universe (thank heavens!) We all have different interests and needs and skills. One person may be more into divination and doing psychic readings. Another may be more into working with energy and shifting the reality around her. A third may be into making items and gadgets that help him to have a better life.

And that's all good. What a boring Universe it would be if we all did the same things.

That means that, as you fair forth into the world of metaphysics, you not only need a plan that works for you financially; you also need a plan that works for your own unique skills and needs and interests. It needs to be affordable, yes, but it also needs to be right for you.

That's one reason this book covers a wide range of different types of metaphysics. Not everything here will be right for you. Not everything will be a good fit. By offering a range of options, you can pick and choose what's right for you. Think of it as an all you can eat buffet where you don't have to put everything on your plate.

So how do you know what's right for you? The same way that you would for any other area of interest in your life. You do your research, and you listen to your own instincts. You look for what speaks to you.

Research is important. Interested in alternative healing, or energywork, or healing? Look at books on the subject. Do a search online. Talk to people, especially people you already know. Look for introduction classes or free talks on the subject, so you can get a feel both for the topic itself and for that teacher.

But, most of all, trust your intuition. Everyone has intuition. It's that hunch you have to take a different route home from work. It's that feeling you have that makes you read the fine print more closely. It's that impression you have that that perfectly nice guy is still not someone you want to be alone with. The problem is that most of us have never been taught how to listen to or trust our intuition, and so we need to learn from scratch.

Most of us have ways our intuition tries to talk to us. The hair standing up on the back of the neck when there's danger. The muscle relaxation when we're safe or with someone we can trust. The unsettled feeling when there's something "going on" but we "can't put our finger on it". The butterflies in the stomach when we're afraid or overwhelmed, even if we can't figure out why.

A lot of these intuitive messages first surface as physical sensations. To learn to tap into your intuition, start listening to what your body is saying.

How do you physically feel when:

- You're safe?
- You're in danger?
- Someone is not being honest with you?
- Something is wrong?
- You're overwhelmed?

Becoming aware of these symptoms can not only help you to be better able to sort out what metaphysical practices are the best for you. It'll also start you on the road to better communication with and use of your intuition, which is another core skill in metaphysics.

There's a lot of different practices, teachers and items in metaphysics. Some are right for you. Some are great but not what you specifically need. And some are just garbage, designed to separate you from your money.

It's kind of like any other field. No matter what you're looking at, whether its groceries or sporting goods or metaphysics, there are always people selling decent products you'd be glad to have, and also dishonest folks, selling things that don't work.

Lucky you. If you work with your intuition, you'll have a head start in being able to weed out the good things that you need from the garbage that's a rip-off (and you can do this in other fields besides metaphysics)

Look at the item. Touch it if you can. Then ignore the advertising, peer pressure or big claims. How does it make you feel? Do you feel confident and relaxed? Do you feel irritated and repelled? Do you get what I think of as a "yes!" feeling?

The kind of feelings you get will give you a heads up to whether this class, practice or item is one that should be a part of your personal plan. Don't make your choices based on this alone, (I'm a big fan of involving both logic and intuition in my life) but factor it in when you're figuring out which direction you should be going in metaphysics.

And keep in mind that your personal plan may grow or change as you go along.

So what kind of metaphysics should you be doing and what shouldn't you be going near at all? That's not hard. Just listen to your intuition and go in the direction that it pulls you, and you'll find that you end up where you need to go.

Part Two

The Magick
of Frugality
and the Frugality
of Magick

Chapter 5
Metaphysical Finances

We've talked about the basics in metaphysics. Now it's time to talk about some of the basics of saving money in metaphysics. Believe it or not, saving money in metaphysics is pretty similar to saving money in any other area of your life, whether it's buying groceries or a car or a summer vacation or a college education. Just like in any other area, there are expensive options and there are more affordable options and there are options that are amazingly cheap or even free.

How do you find those options?

- You do your research.
- You know your options.
- You make connections
- You watch for discounts.

And then you shop. Shop for the product and the price that best meets your needs.

Keep in mind that, just as at the grocery store, price is not the only thing to consider. Your budget is important, yes, and your ability to stretch that budget to the most knowledge and tools and options you can- but sometimes you'll have to balance price with other factors.

Sometimes durability and how long something will hold up is important. Sometimes how much use you'll get out of something. Sometimes a tool will have just the right feel in your hand, or the color or appearance of it will make you feel good every time you see or touch it (and thereby improve the vibration of your energy field.)

It really is like shopping at the supermarket. Sometimes you buy the house brand because milk is milk. Sometimes you go for a particular name brand, because the flavor of those particular cookies is worth an extra fifty cents. And sometimes you can do without Brussels sprouts this week (and maybe this lifetime...)

You consider your budget. You know what's a good buy and what's not. You do the least expensive thing when it doesn't matter to you and maybe use what you've saved to spend a little more on things where it does.

Because this is really all about you. Your budget. Your plan. Your journey into metaphysics. So you're the one who gets to decide what you spend your money on and what you don't.

And this book is just here to give you more information so you can make those choices.

More information coming up on how to make your money go further in metaphysics.

Chapter 6
Doing Your Research

In the last chapter, we talked about how smart shopping in the metaphysical world is like smart shopping in any other area of your life. Just like going to the grocery store, the first step in shopping smart is to know your subject.

- What's a normal price? What's a good price? What's a jacked up price?
- Is this a real sale, or have they jacked up the price and dropped it to make a "sale"?
- Where do specific items or materials matter? Where are less expensive substitutions workable?
- Where does brand matter? If there are three different versions of something, is there a functional reason why one is preferable to the others?
- What's the history of this particular vendor? Are his customers satisfied with the results?

And this is where research comes in.

Start out by figuring out what kinds of knowledge, tools and experiences you're looking for. You'll want to learn what kinds of options there are. You'll also need to figure out which ones matter to you and which ones don't.

- Do you need beeswax candles, or will the ones you already have be sufficient?
- Are emeralds necessary for a prosperity working, or will any green stone do the job?

- Do you need the four volume encyclopedia of meditation, or will the hundred page paperback be enough to get you started?
- If there are two classes on the same topic, which teacher teaches in a way that works better for you?

Once you know what you want, and the particulars about what matters to you and what doesn't, start your research on the internet. Search for the items you want, and get a feel for the kind of prices you're looking at. Learn how much they cost at different places and times so that you know what's a bargain and what's not.

Sign up for mailing lists at places that carry what you want so useful information will flow to you.

With this basic information, now check out local shops and other resources. Make a list of new age centers, wiccan stores, rock shops and nature facilities (often good sources for crystals). Check local libraries for talks that connect with your metaphysical interests. These talks offer information, and can also be a good place to meet teachers and other people interested in metaphysical topics. Librarians are also good sources of assorted information. Keep adult education programs in mind. Many offer alternative health and divination classes. Visit and find out which ones are a good match for you and what you're trying to do.

This is the time to start to make connections, too. A good metaphysical shop tends to offer not only products, but also service, information, classes and support. Community is an added value, especially when you're getting started. Make friends with the shop owners who feel like a good match to you.

A local shop also offers you the chance to see an item in person, pick it up and feel how its energy fits with yours. There's a lot of variability in metaphysical tools and supplies, and the ability to check the energy in person makes it more likely that you will end up with something that actually resonates with your energy.

Prices are sometimes less online, but even if the price is slightly higher, I find it's worth it to support the local metaphysical store that will tell me which stones I might like or how to clear bad energy out of my house, and who let me check the energy of an item before I buy it.

Once you've know what you want and what are reasonable prices for those things, keep an eye out for discounts and specials. Some shops have a frequent shopper program or a "buy two, get one" sale. Some stores just charge more for certain things.

Watch for free or inexpensively priced introduction talks or classes. These let you get a feel for a topic or a teacher for a small investment, and decide whether it's right for you without laying out a lot of money.

To summarize:

- Know what you want.
- Know what features matter to you (and what ones don't.)
- Know what the standard prices are, and
- Know where the best prices are.

With those four points, you'll be the best position to shop in metaphysics and get the best value for your money.

Chapter 7
Finding Your Tribe

You've done your basic research, you know what you want, and you have more of an idea about what's available in your area and sphere of influence.

Now it's time for the next step.

You need to network. Connect. Find your people.

This includes looking at:

- Online groups;
- Online chat groups;
- Facebook pages and web groups for authorities in areas you want to know more about;
- Spiritual groups, covens and congregations;
- Metaphysical conventions;
- New Age or metaphysical stores;
- Alternative health and metaphysical classes, in metaphysical facilities or in more mainstream options, such as adult education programs.

You know that old song about "looking for love in all the wrong places"? Well, you need to look for magick in all of the right places- the places where your kind of metaphysical people hang out.

You've made a list of possibilities from your research. Now narrow it down a bit by looking at what you're trying to learn/do/ accomplish and seeing if a group is a good match for that. Is what they're doing the same as what you want to do? Barring that, is there a good overlap, so that being with them may help you to move forwards on your own path?

Then visit. Sample. Get to know people.

No one is the perfect fit with everyone else. Some people and some groups are open to all, and some are not but may be a good match for you, nonetheless. Some groups are more closed or insular, and you may or may not be the right fit for them.

You may also find that a particular group is not a good fit for you, but that there may be individuals in that group who have something to offer you (or that you have something to offer to.) Keep that in mind when you're looking around.

Think of it as being like dating- only metaphysical...

When you find groups that you like, be sure to get on their mailing lists and check out their web presence, so that you'll know what's going on with them that you might want to be a part of.

So, what kinds of benefits come out of the human side of metaphysics?

- Many groups have free classes.
- Many shops offer affordable introduction classes, which let you get a feel for a particular practice before you invest a lot of time or money in them.
- Many conventions offer a large assortment of different types of classes for one relatively affordable price.
- Experts- shops, conventions and groups all have the potential to include people who are fascinated by a particular type of metaphysics- and many of these are glad to talk about their area if you approach

them respectfully.

- Many groups, whether live or online, offer opportunities to discuss different metaphysical topics. Many things in metaphysics have multiple approaches, and it's good to get a look at how different people approach a single topic.
- Groups tend to contain people who have followed the same path that you're presently on. It's useful, when you run up against a question or a challenge, to have someone you can ask for advice.
- Groups often offer chances to barter for other supplies or skills, metaphysical or otherwise. This could mean exchanging books for a class, or swopping a batch of your really good brownies for a great crystal.
- Groups may give you the chance to split the price of a bulk purchase or share an expensive item.
- And finally, it feels really good to find your tribe. To find people who speak the language, understand what you're doing and don't think you're crazy because you're not limiting yourself to things in the physical world. It feels good, and it's healthy to have a support group that gets you, a group where you belong.

When you're looking for your tribe, take into account not only what the group is about, (Are they Reiki practitioners? Wiccans? Esoteric tinkerers?) but also the energy of the group and the individuals of the group. When you meet them, do you feel comfortable and welcome? Some feelings of separateness are natural when you first meet people, but if the group doesn't feel good to you or you continue to feel like an outsider long after you've first met them, you may need to evaluate whether you and this group connect well, or whether you should keep moving.

It's also worth noting that, with few exceptions, you're not limited to belonging to only one group. I have a number of different esoteric groups that I associate with, each one different, special and having its own strengths and weaknesses. For most groups, you also have the right to choose how much or how little you want to be involved.

At that point, your group presence is determined by how much time and effort you want to put into the community- and, like everything else on your esoteric journey, that is something uniquely up to you.

Chapter 8
Conferences, Festivals and Fairs

In the last chapter, we talked about networking, making human connections and finding your tribe. In this chapter, we'll look at one particular type of networking – metaphysical conferences, festivals and fairs.

There's a big variety of metaphysical get-togethers out there. Some are focused on one particular area of metaphysics, like reading tarot or accupressure. Some are more general and incorporate a big assortment of different topics. Some are out in nature. Some are held in hotels. Some are small and cozy. Some are enormous. Some are primarily educational. Some are commercial. And some are any or all of the above.

And one of the biggest variables of all is that of price- anything from triple digits (or more) to a can of food for the local food pantry.

This chapter is less about picking out a gathering. That's a matter of individual choice. This chapter is more about different ways to control costs when you hit a convention.

To find a con or festival, be aware of what's going on around you. Check online, in newsletters, and in local alternative health and metaphysical magazines for what's happening in your area. If there's a print or online listing, check out what presentations and vendors will be there, and look at whether the cost will be balanced by how much of it is of interest to you.

And to better manage your budget:

- Plan ahead. Many gatherings have early registration discounts which make membership more affordable.
- See if there are other discounts you qualify for. Some events offer discounts to groups such as students, the military or senior citizens.
- Check to see if there are other ways you can get money off. Many cons will offer money off of your registration for teaching or volunteering. (Arrange this in advance.)
- Carpool. Save the environment and some bucks at the same time.
- Is this con close to where you live? Staying at home and day tripping saves you the cost of a hotel room.
- Is this con further away? If you need to stay over, finding someone to split the room fee cuts costs.
- Or, if you can't get a roommate, many times staying at the hotel down the street is less convenient, but more affordable.
- Have a budget. You're less likely to spend too much money on tempting items if you pick an amount of money in advance and stick to it.
- Food at a hotel during a con is often expensive. Eat a solid meal before entering. If it's permitted, bring a sandwich in a cooler bag, rather than paying an inflated price for roughly the same thing.

Most of all, plan to get the most value possible out of any gathering that you attend. If the schedule's posted in advance, look it over and plan what presentations you want to attend. When you're there, talk to the vendors. Most of them are passionate about what they stock, and, while they're there to sell things, many of them will also explain about what they offer and how you can incorporate it into your unique practice. (I've learned a lot of things that way.) If you have free time, hang out in central areas and talk to any people who are open to conversation. Many times you can learn a lot that way too.

A good metaphysical gathering is like a wonderful metaphysical "all-you can eat" buffet, with a lot of information and resources all brought together in place for your convenience. To get the best value out of it, plan in advance, find ones that are a match for your journey, and find ways to save money on things that don't matter to you, so you have it for things that do.

Part Three

The Metaphysical Buffet

Chapter 9
Beginning Meditation

When looking at affordable types of metaphysics, meditation is a great place to start. Different kinds of meditation are part of the spiritual and cultural practices of almost every culture throughout history. Whether it's introspective prayer, chanting, moving meditations or incorporating meditation in the things that you do every day, meditation is a powerful tool for calming the mind, finding your center, supporting your health and connecting with your own spirituality.

So, what is meditation? At its most basic level, meditation is using focus to calm the mind and clear it of stress and chatter; and there are as many ways to meditate as there are people to do them.

Meditation started out as a spiritual practice, and is still powerful in this capacity. In addition, modern studies find that meditation is helpful in supporting health in body, mind and spirit. Meditation can decrease stress and increase emotional resilience, helping with such challenges as anxiety and depression. It can help you manage stress better, which means lower blood pressure and less risk of heart attack and stroke. It supports the immune system, which not only means less colds but also less serious diseases.

While not a wonder drug, regular meditation seems to have an overall positive effect on your health, well-being and quality of life. It's not that hard either. A traditional meditation practice involved meditating for substantial times a day, but studies are finding that even small amounts of meditation, when done regularly, have a positive effect on your health and well being. (Longer periods have a greater effect, but even a small amount such as five to ten minutes will help- and that's good news for those of us with schedules already stretched at the seams.)

Let's look a little more closely at meditation.

There are many different types of meditation, but there are certain elements that they have in common. Keep these in mind, whether you're doing relaxation, focusing on a candle, or doing a moving meditation to clear your mind.

First, minimize distractions. Most meditations involve putting your focus on one thing at a time and clearing your mind of all other "chatter", so an environment that weeds out as many distractions as possible makes it easier to enter a state of meditation.

Find a quiet place to meditate. Send your roommates to the movies. Turn off the TV and take the phone off the hook. Draw the drapes to cut down on visual distractions.

Some people like to meditate in total silence. Others like some kind of "white noise', whether it's the sounds of nature or quiet soothing music, to sooth the brain into a relaxed state. Try them both to find out which works best for you.

Make sure that you won't be interrupted while you meditate. Make sure that you're in a comfortable position with your body supported. (Your leg going to sleep or your head bobbing can startle you out of your meditation.)

Remember that the goal of meditation is to relax your mind and focus on one thing. Do your best to put other things aside while you meditate.

Then relax and enjoy…

The number one concern that most beginning meditators have is "What if I get distracted?" They're worried about something called "the monkey mind", (called this because of the brain's tendency to chatter distractingly like a monkey.)

When most people start meditating, they're able to calm their minds for a second or two, and then those other thoughts begin to intrude. Politics. What they're having for lunch that day. The latest uproar online. Their to-do list.

Many beginners try to meditate but can't keep their focus, and end up giving up because they can't stop the mental chatter. That's actually pretty silly. If you were learning gymnastics, or algebra, or rocket science, you wouldn't expect to be perfect first time, right? Somehow, people seem to think that, since they've had a mind all of their lives, they should be better at controlling their thoughts.

Don't let the monkey mind scare you. Like anything else, it takes practice to get good at meditation, but even a beginner's meditation has positive effects for body, mind and spirit.

What's the best way to deal with the monkey mind? Most people make the mistake of trying to force those distractions out of their mind. Unfortunately, the more you fight those thoughts, the harder they'll stick.

Instead, try the cloud technique.

When you meditate, if a distracting thought pops up, don't fight it. Instead, acknowledge it. "Oh, there's another thought."

Picture it drifting across your mind like a cloud and on out of sight, and return your focus to your meditation. Avoiding mental struggle makes it easier to stay in meditation.

When you're meditating, distracting thoughts are like unhappy children that want your attention. If you try to send them away, they'll just clutch at you and cry louder, but if you acknowledge them and say that you'll deal with them once your meditation period is over (and if you keep that promise), they'll tend to give you space to do your meditation.

Let's start with one of the most basic of meditation techniques- focusing on the breath. A breathing meditation can be done while seated with your eyes closed, but it can also be done with your eyes open while walking or running.

Breathe in through your nose and out through your mouth. Breathe slowly and deeply, filling your lungs as much as you can, holding the breath a couple of seconds, and then blowing out the breath, emptying your lungs as fully as possible. Breathe in and out, fully filling your lungs and fully emptying them.

As you breathe, focus totally on the breath. Focus on what it feels like to breathe deeply. Focus on what it feels like as you empty your lungs.

If you find your mind wandering, gently but firmly return to focusing on the breath, as we discussed earlier in this chapter. There's time enough to think about other things once you're through meditation.

Do your breathing meditation for one minute, five minutes, twenty minutes- whatever time you have for meditation. When you feel your body start to relax, you'll know the meditation is doing its job. More is better, but even a short time has its benefits.

Next, let's do a classic whole body relaxation. Settle yourself comfortably with your body comfortable and supported. (I find a recliner great for this.)

Close your eyes. We're going to start with deep breathing just as we did in the first meditation. Slowly and deeply. In through the nose and out through the mouth. Focusing on your breathing. Acknowledging any distracting thoughts that come by and letting them drift on like clouds as you return your attention to your breathing.

And as you breathe, picture yourself surrounded by light. Picture yourself, as you breath in, breathing in that light. Breathe that light into each part of your body in turn. Set your intention that, as you breathe light into each part of your body, that part becomes strong and healthy, energized and very relaxed. Picture that, as you breathe out, you breathe out any illness, injury, pain or weakness, leaving that part of your body feeling great.

Start by breathing into your feet, then your ankles, then your legs. Work your way up your body, through back, stomach, and chest, through hands, arms and shoulders, through neck and head.

Take your time about this. Focus on your breathing

and how your body feels as you do this. Notice how it feels strong and energized and just plain wonderful.

And when you've breathed light into every part of your body, you can end the meditation and open your eyes, or move on to another metaphysical practice, now that you are focused, energized and feel great.

For a more active experience, try a meditation snack. Choose a small food item, like a strawberry or a piece of chocolate.

Settle yourself comfortably in a time and place that is free of distractions. Take a deep breath and relax. Prepare yourself to focus on the experience of eating. We're going to focus totally on all of the sensory experiences that are part of eating. (You know- the ones we usually ignore because we're so busy thinking about twenty different things.)

Pick up your strawberry. What does it feel like in your hand? Is it smooth or textured, heavy or light? Take a moment and really feel the weight of it in your hand.

Look at your strawberry. What color is it? Sure, it's red, but what color of red? Is it more than one shade? And what about the colors of the stem and other markings? What shape is it? Turn it over and look at it from different angles. What does it look like when you look at it from a different side?

Hold it close to your nose and smell it. Is there an aroma to your strawberry? Tangy or sweet? What does it smell like?

This is your strawberry. Take some time to really

get to know it- and then, when you're ready, it's time to take a bite.

Pay attention to what you feel as you bite into the strawberry. Feel the resistance of the outside of it and how it's different from the texture of the inner pulp. Feel the juice of the strawberry dance in your mouth. What does the juice taste like? Is the taste different from the pulp and from the outside of the strawberry?

Concentrate of the smell of the strawberry again. Is it different now that the fruit is in your mouth?

Nibble your strawberry and be conscious of each little bite. How are they different? How are they the same?

Being conscious of your food as you eat is one way of accessing the benefits of meditation- and I'll bet it will also be the best strawberry or piece of chocolate you've ever eaten.

Meditation is free, and there are lots of free resources online to help you meditate.

Search for

- Instructions for different kinds of meditations, such as the three that I included in this chapter.
- Meditation music and recordings to help you to relax your mind.
- Meditation blogs and websites with resources to help you learn to meditate.
- Meditation environments, where you can meditate together with people all over the internet.

Not every resource will be right for you, but there's a wide variety of options available to help you build your own individual meditation practice.

It's easy. It's free. It's flexible and forgiving. It takes as much or as little time as you have to give it. There's lots of different ways to do it. It has positive effects on your health in body, mind and spirit. And it feels great.

Meditation. What's not to love?

If you can only pick one of the many affordable types of metaphysics we'll be talking about in this book, I'd seriously recommend that you choose meditation as the tool that can do you the most good. We've only touched on a few types of meditation here, but there's a whole lot of different types out there waiting for you to make friends with them. Find books, go online, take classes and, above all, try different methods of meditation until you find the one or ones that work best for you.

And then, practice regularly. Every day, if you can. Do the amount of time that feels good to you.

And try not to consider it as "one more darned thing" you need to squeeze into your schedule. Think about it instead as a treat that you're giving yourself. It really does feel good if you're willing to be present with it, even for only a few minutes, and it'll renew your energy to go out and have a better day.

We've looked at meditation. In the next chapter, we'll be building on this with its cousin, visualization.

See you there.

Chapter 10
Visualization

In the last chapter, we talked about meditation and some of the benefits you can get from it for free. In this chapter, we're going to talk about visualization.

Visualization is a specific type of meditation that focuses on creating and holding a mental image. It's often done with the intention of maintaining or improving a skill, or for manifesting something that's not currently in a person's life. Visualization has been used by athletes to boost their performance. It's been used by people with physical limitations to help with recovery. It's been used by prisoners of war to keep physically and mentally fit.

And you can use it, too.

The basic steps in visualization are:

- Position yourself comfortably, so you can focus on your visualization.
- Close your eyes.
- Relax. (One way to do this is the whole body relaxation from chapter 9 Beginning Meditation.)
- Form an image in your mind of what you're trying to achieve.
- See things happening now, not "going to happen".
- Put yourself in the visualization. (Don't see a car, see yourself driving that car.)
- It's called visualization, but it works better if you include as many of the five senses as possible. What does your goal sound like? Feel like?
- A visualization is also stronger when you include

feeling. (Don't picture yourself driving a car-picture yourself feeling **great** driving a car.) Sometimes just visualizing feeling great is enough to bring good things into your life.

- Hold that image for as long as you can or have time to.
- Repeat when you can.

That's it. There's lots of different ways to vary this process, but those are the basic core pieces of visualization. It's a time tested and generally useful method of using intention and focus to change the nature of reality around you; and in keeping with the focus of this book, it's absolutely free.

Chapter 11
The Power of Prayer

Some people are religious, making a connection with the Divine through some form of organized religion. Some people are spiritual, connecting with the Divine directly without a formal structure. Some are both. Some are neither. Some people worship a god, or a goddess, or a concept of a divine creator. Some worship more than one. And some choose none of the above.

If you come from the neither or none of the above parts of life, this chapter may not have as much to give you, but if you have a regular prayer practice, it's worth noting that this is also metaphysical, since it is a non-physical way of interacting with and affecting the nature of reality.

And prayer works. Studies have found that:

- People with a regular prayer practice often enjoy the same health and stress management benefits as people who meditate on an ongoing basis.
- A regular prayer practice has been associated with increased mental and emotional resilience and coping strategies.
- This stress management and emotional resilience prevents emotional exhaustion, which puts people in the position to make better decisions and have better lives.
- People who are prayed for recover from surgery faster and require less pain medication (and this is true for people who don't even know they're being prayed for.)

- Prayer also has a strong correlation with remission, recovery and survival rates in folks with serious illnesses such as cardiac problems, cancer and AIDS.

Overall, prayer has a lot going for it.

Prayer is a spiritual act- a connection between you and the Divine as you experience it. On beyond that, from a metaphysical standpoint, the Divine invites us to be co-creators in this world, and prayer is one way that we can do this.

There are lots of different kinds of prayers out there, but I'm mainly going talking about four different varieties from a metaphysical standpoint.

- Prayers of praise.
- Prayers of petition- where you're asking for something for yourself.
- Prayers of intercession- where you're asking for something for someone else.
- Prayers of thanks.

Prayers of Praise- are prayers that acknowledge everything that is working or is good in your life, and acknowledges the Creator who made that happen.

Metaphysically, by putting your focus on what's positive, you raise your energy levels to more positive ones, and that tends to attract or create more positive people, things and experiences in your life.

Prayers of Petition and Prayers of Intercession- These two types of prayer are similar to each other. The main difference between them is whether you are asking for something for yourself (petition) or something for someone else (intercession).

Either way, the act of asking puts your focus on a desired outcome, whether you're asking for something specific or "Thy Will be done." Metaphysically, by focusing your attention, you increase the odds of having it happen.

Prayers of Thanks- These are similar to prayers of praise, in that they express gratitude for something in your life, but they're more acknowledgements of thanks for divine help.

From a metaphysical standpoint, once again focus on what's good and gratitude for it raises our energy, and attracts more blessings into our lives.

One thing to be clear about though- prayer is not like a vending machine where you put prayer in and a prize pops out. When you pray, you're asking for help from someone bigger than us all who can see the big picture that we can't- and that means that, even with a loving diety, sometimes the answer has to be "No."

That being said, prayer repeatedly shows positive effects in the lives of those who practice it.

Some other options to consider:

- Blessing your meals before eating can improve your life through a positive focus.

- Formal prayers, such as the Lord's Prayer, can be helpful, but informal prayers are also a good thing. If you're in distress, don't worry about the impression you might make- just talk to your creator with words from your heart. He won't mind- He knew who you were when He made you.
- Try developing a prayer chain to have multiple people praying for those in need in times of challenge. Interestingly enough, a prayer chain can contain people of different spiritual paths and still be effective in helping those in need.

The bottom line is that prayer is a good thing, no matter what spiritual path you follow- and the prayer that works best is the one that comes from your heart.

Chapter 12
Working With Sound

Sound is a powerful tool for clearing problem energy and generating good. In Feng Shui, bells clear stuck energy and wind chimes remove negative. Karuna Reiki uses chanting and toning (two different vocal techniques) to clear problem energy, including blockages and chronic complaints "stuck" in the body itself. Sounds like clapping, stamping or other sharp noises have been used in magick to disrupt or disperse bad fortune and clear occupied areas.

How's this work? From a wyrd science standpoint, energy is made up of vibrational waves. Since sound is also made of vibrational waves, it can be used to shift energy from an adverse form to a more positive one. When two types of waves come together, "entrainment" causes one to gradually shift into phase with the other. You hold the desired sound until the negative energy is interrupted, reforming in a more harmonious form.

Let's look at metaphysical ways to work with sound.

Chanting is a cross cultural spiritual practice, using the rhythmic speaking or singing of words or sounds, often on one or two notes. It can be used for:

- Focus,
- Meditation,
- Clearing the mind,
- Stress management,
- Spiritual development,

And a lot of other things as well.

You can also listen to recordings of chanting, and get some of the effects of actually chanting for yourself.

Because chanting is so widely done across cultures and throughout history, there are lots of different ways to chant. Do some research and listen to different kinds of chanting to find the variety that speaks most to you.

Most of our beliefs, whether positive or negative, are created by being told the same things over and over, whether by someone else or by ourselves. An affirmation is a positive statement used to replace a negative belief. Repeating affirmations creates new, positive programming and forces old negative beliefs out. Research indicates that it takes approximately 1000 repetitions to replace a negative belief with a positive one. Seems like a lot until you look at the "No"s said to the average toddler, and realize that that's about 2 1/2 days' worth....

And many people start to feel results with 200 repetitions or less.

There are guidelines that make an affirmation work better:

- It's positive ("I'm graceful" not "I'm not clumsy");
- It's happening now ("I'm healthy" not "I will be healthy");
- It's easy to say (no tongue twisters);
- It's better if it's shorter ("I sleep well" not "I sleep deeply without tossing and turning");
- It's more powerful if it's said with emotion.

That's the basics. Sounds simple, right? Too simple, maybe? But the truth is that affirmations work. Even if you don't say them 1000 times.

Affirmations have great power:

- to change your beliefs;
- to attract more positive things;
- to improve the effects of your mind-body connection;
- to improve your health, and mind-set, and ability to live your dreams.

One of the most popular methods to clear problem energy is smudging. Classic smudging involves circulating smoke from smoldering plants, most frequently sage, to clear negative energy.

Classic sage smudging is simple and effective, but also has some problems. The aroma lingers, which may not be welcome. The smoke may be poorly tolerated by folks with respiratory issues and may trigger smoke detectors and sprinkler systems. Because of my own wheezy lungs, I was pleased when I learned how to smudge with sound. You can learn how to do this too.

First, what kind of sound? Your choice may vary, based on the kind of space, energetic issues and your personal preferences. If it's your own private home, you have more options than if you're clearing a cubicle or meeting room at work. A space shared by others, especially non-magickal folks, may require the discretion of wind chimes, the stomping of "a foot that has gone to sleep" or appropriate music on a desk radio. A more private area is open to drumming, rattles, chanting or singing bowls.

Your sound choice may also depend on the degree

of the problem. A slight after-cloud from a visit from a snippy cousin may be cleared by clapping your hands a half dozen times in the space she infested, while clearing the energy left by the skanky roommate who maxed out your credit cards, stole your boyfriend and disappeared, leaving you to field inquiries from the police may take an entire Tibetan brass band.

Finally, personal preference plays into this. To make energy more harmonious for you, it's not bad to choose sounds you find harmonious, keeping in mind that some cases may do better with other sounds. Some things need a feather, but sometimes you just need a crowbar. Know that the sound needed to clear problem energy is not always pleasant or harmonious. Follow your intuition in what kind of sound is needed.

It's helpful before you clear problem energy to try to get your own energy in a good space.

Sound smudging has three stages: evaluation, treatment and re-evaluation. You can do three or more circuits of the room, one for each stage, or you can combine them, checking for problem energy as you move through the room, stopping to clear problem spots, then re-evaluating before moving on. Choose a point like the main doorway as your start and end. I usually work widdershins (counter-clockwise) for banishing bad energy and sunwards (clockwise) for summoning good. If you can't walk around the walls, stand in the center and turn in the appropriate direction while sending sound throughout all of the room.

From your start point, move in your chosen direction, continuously making your sound and listening carefully. Does the sound change key, drop in volume, sound muddy or off? Sound will shift, frequently in unpleasant ways, in areas of problem energy. If the whole room's energy is a problem, you may have to test your sound in another room or outside to hear it in healthy energy. To double check, back out of the possible problem area and re-enter with your sound to see if it shifts again.

Many times, continuing to pour sound into the area with the intention that the negative energy will return to a positive state is all you need to do. The sound will return to normal as the energy entrains and comes into harmony with it. In some cases wherein the problem energy is persistent, more extreme measures may be needed.

To correct stubborn energy, start with sharp, strong sounds, such as clapping, striking a bowl, drum or gong, sharp vocal sounds like "HUH!" or stamping, followed quickly by a continuous sound such as singing a bowl, humming or playing a non-percussive instrument. Sharp sounds disrupt the problem vibrations, leaving them more open to harmonious entrainment.

Last, re-evaluate the energy. Recheck the sound in areas that previously had problems. Does the sound stay normal now, or is there still shift? If you've only partially cleared the energy, the sound will tell you.

You might wish to bless your space then or flood it with positive energy. Nature abhors a vacuum and it is better not to leave an opening for negative energy to return

Once your energy is cleared, enjoy.

These are three of the biggest ways to work with sound in metaphysics, but there are a lot more out there. These three have the advantage of being very affordable, because they only require the equipment that you were born with, and they don't need much practice to get started in.

Remember that sound is often an important tool in many metaphysical practices. The key is to find out what kind of sound is right for you.

Chapter 13
On Divination

Divination is a term for the collective methods of doing psychic readings. Psychic readings give you information through your own natural intuition, also known as "the sixth sense" (because it uses senses beyond the physical five we're all familiar with.)

I don't know if everyone is psychic. I haven't met everyone yet; but from my experience, it seems to me that everyone has at least a certain amount of natural latent psychic ability. You see traces of it when:

- You think about someone you haven't talked to for awhile and then they call you.
- You get a song stuck in your head, turn on the radio and hear it playing.
- You "have a feeling" and take an alternative route home from work and find you've missed an accident.

That sort of thing. That's the intuition that you don't know you have popping out and trying to get your attention.

And all methods of divination, whether cards or stars or tea leaves, are just systems that you use for getting in touch with the natural intuition that's in your head and your heart and your spirit. The more you learn to listen to that inner voice, the better you'll get at hearing it and the more use it can be to you.

We'll be talking about some different methods of

divination in this section, and ways to do it affordably, but first I'd like to go into three core concepts that apply to all of the different types of readings.

The first is the concept of Free Will. We all have Free Will, the ability to make choices, whether good, bad or indifferent; and, by choosing, to have a certain amount of control over our lives. This means that the future is not fixed, because at any moment, we can choose to change the direction of our lives and head off into a new future.

At that point, what a good reading does is to tell you if you keep on doing things the way you've been doing them, here's where you're going- and if you don't want to go there, you now know you need to change your direction in life. There is no "Doom". There is no "Fate". There are only choices, and information helps you make better ones. It's important for you to know this yourself, and it's also important, if you read for others, to let them know that too.

Don't build any self fulfilling prophesies. Just give yourself and others the information they need for the adventure of life, and the knowledge that they can always change where they're going.

The second is the concept of whether you can read for yourself or not. Some people think you can't read for yourself. Some people think you can. My experience is that, whether you believe you can or you can't, either way you're probably right. Since intent (belief) shapes reality, you're going to tend to get the results you believe in. (Something to think about when you chose what you believe.)

I believe that I can read for myself and have found that to be the case with one key proviso. I find that, the more important or high stakes the question I'm reading about, the more likely I am to tell myself what I want to hear…and that is not always the most accurate information.

It's a human thing. No one wants to hear bad news, especially on something important. Even good psychics are as capable of kidding themselves as any other people. For that reason, if it's a low to medium level question (ex: "What's the best use of my time tomorrow?"), I'll do my own reading, but if it's something I've got a lot of stress about (ex: "Should I go through with surgery at this time?") I'll get a reading from another psychic, preferably one who doesn't have any stake in the outcome. That's going to give me the most accurate information possible, to use as part of making good choices in my life.

Last, if you're getting a reading from someone else, please keep in mind:

- No reader is the right reader for everyone. If you don't feel a connection, look for someone else.
- No reader is perfect 100% of the time.
- Sometimes a reading won't make sense right away. If you hear something that doesn't make sense to you, keep it in mind (because it may make sense later on.)
- Most readers are good folks, but some are not. If a reader is putting you down, making you afraid, or trying to get you to give them large sums of money beyond what was agreed on for the reading, please excuse yourself and don't go back.

Trust your feelings, and choose the reader who feels

right for you.

That being said, here's a couple of ways that you can bring divination into your life and still not break the budget.

- Do your own readings, where appropriate. - This is assuming that a) you believe you can read for yourself, b) the issue is low key enough that you won't tell yourself what you want to hear, and c) you've got enough practice doing your method of reading to get workable results. (Start practicing on small things so you know what you're doing when you want to do a reading on something more important.)
- Get a reading from a friend. - To do this, you'll want some idea of how good your friend is at doing readings.
- Swop readings.- When you have gained some experience in doing readings, you may have someone offering to swop readings with you.

All of these methods are fine with a person who's good at doing readings, and who's a good match for you. For more serious subjects, you may want to look for a professional reader who feels like a good match for you.

And now, let's get to some specific types of divination.

Chapter 14
Omens, Portents and Signs

Omens, signs and portents. Three words for a way of doing readings that goes as far back as history does.

From the dawn of time, men and women have looked around them for signs to tell them what's happening next in their lives- and they've been finding them.

Some of these signs have been more physical, like birds chattering in my backyard when a big storm is coming or the classic "red sky at morning, sailor take warning." Some, however, fall more in the metaphysical end of things, being omens that have no logical mundane connection with the event they predict. An itchy palm meaning money coming in. Dropping a knife meaning a man is coming to visit. The sight of a comet heralding a birth, death or other event of importance.

Many traditional omens can be found in modern superstitions. You can research them yourself, and use that knowledge to have a better feel for where life is taking you.

Or, you can look around and see what personal omens are happening in your own life. Pay attention to what's happening around you, especially to little things. Dropping your phone. A song on the radio. Finding a coin in your path. A bumper sticker on the car ahead of you. Especially look for things that seem odd or out of place, or that resonate with a question or issue in your life.

And watch for the events that seem to happen after you've seen your omen. What is that bumper sticker or song or dropped phone telling you is going to happen?

I live in a suburban neighborhood, but every once in

awhile, we'll spot one of our hidden colony of bunnies out and fearlessly frolicking on our back yard. (Odd, because he is remarkably non-spooky for a rabbit in a neighborhood with plenty of traffic in free ranging cats, dogs and people.) Whenever we see "da bunny", that's a sign that something delightful will happen within the next 24 hours.

So, what's your "bunny"? Take note of patterns and things that seem to correspond, even if they at first seem unconnected. If you're finding a regular pattern, you may have just spotted one of your personal omens. And trust your intuition- many times, an omen will make your skin tingle, the hair on the back of your neck standup or give you some other alert to pay attention to what's happening.

With more experience at watching for omens, you'll even get to the point where you can ask to receive one. Gotta question, challenge or area of concern? At night, as you drop off to sleep, ask that, the following day, you'll receive an omen of what's coming, or of what's your best choice. Be sure to include the key concepts that:

- It comes in a way that you will notice,
- It comes in a way that is positive for you, and
- It comes in a clear and easy to understand form.

This may not work the first time that you try it, but, with practice, you'll find that you can get answers on request using this method. This is a form of dream programming and can be a very helpful tool for you.

You're surrounded by omens, signs and portents. Once you look and learn your own language of symbols, you'll find the world has a lot of things to tell you.

Chapter 15
Interpreting Dreams

Most human beings seem to have at least a touch of latent psychic ability. For many of us, dreams are where it first pops up to say "hi!" I don't know how many people I've talked to who confess to "funny dreams" or ask if they're crazy because they dream something that later actually happens.

There's a reason for that.

Your mind is split into two parts- the conscious and the unconscious. Your unconscious mind includes about 85% of the power of the mind, including the mind- body connection, unconscious beliefs and most of your untrained psychic ability. It's like a trusting three year old- it believes everything that you tell it and will try its best to make it true, whether it originally was or not.

Your conscious mind, on the other hand, has about 15% of the power of the brain and includes your judgment. Judgment tries its best to protect you and keep you safe. That's good when it's telling you to not touch the hot stove or not take a ride from the creepy stranger. It's not so good when it's trying to protect you from standing out or looking funny by telling you things like "There's no such thing as psychic ability.", "People will think you're weird." or "Who are you to think you're so special?" All of these are "helpful" attempts to protect you that end up making you ignore or deny your natural psy.

That's where dreaming comes in. When you're awake, your judgment is awake too, keeping you safe from "being psychic"; but when you go to sleep, your judgment goes to sleep, but your unconscious stays up and parties in your dreams. That's why, for many folks, dreams are the first inkling they get of a sense beyond the basic five.

Not all dreams are psychic- but some are. You'll know them because they tend to kind of stand out. They feel very real or they stick with you, leaving you thinking about them long after you wake.

Some psychic dreams are literal. You dream of a plane crash and the day after, a plane just like the one in your dreams crashes. Some dreams, on the other hand, are symbolic. Those are a little trickier.

When you're interpreting a symbolic dream, the first thing you need to know is that there are lots of lovely books on dream interpretation out there. The problem is that they don't really work. That's because they're a list of someone else's symbols, and each of us has dreams full of symbols unique to us.

If I had a dream of a cat, that could mean "friendly and comforting", and your dream of a cat might mean "formal and aloof." Both are legitimate interpretations of cats in dreams. The trick is to learn what your symbols are so you can hear what your intuition is trying to tell you through your own dreams.

Here's the way to do that.

When you have a dream that feels significant, as soon as you can, write down everything you can remember about it. Next, look at what you've written, and mark any word or item that seems to jump out at you.

Third, look at the items you've marked and ask yourself the Magick Questions about each one:

- What is (your item here) to me?
  and
- How did (your item here) make me feel?

These questions may seem simple, but they let the light shine onto the symbols in your dream so that you can see them clearly. A dream about a bear may be about hibernating/ sleeping, or about something that comes in threes (like three bears) or something that's "just right." A dream about a scary dog is very different from a dream about a cuddly dog.

Once you've asked the Magick Questions for each of the items you've marked, you'll find that a pattern begins to emerge from the answers. Tell yourself the story that that pattern shows you- the story behind the story of your dream.

And see what your dream is trying to tell you.

This is a very stripped down version of how to do basic dream interpretation. If you want to learn more about this, I've written a book "The Power of Your Psychic Dreams" that gives you more specifics about the process, as well as other ways to use your dreams to access your inner wisdom.

Once you're familiar with the basic process of dream interpretation, you'll find that the more you do it, the better you'll get. You'll find that the more you do it, the more dreams will come. And you'll find the more that you listen to your dreams, the more your intuition will pop up in other ways in your life.

Dream work is not only affordable and doesn't take much in the line of equipment (a pad of paper, a pencil or pen, and a hi-liter). It's also a great way to begin to make contact with your psychic self.

Sweet dreams.

Chapter 16
Dowsing for Answers

One way of doing a simple psychic reading is by dowsing for answers with a pendulum.

What's a pendulum? In its simplest form, a pendulum is any weight hanging from something flexible. You can do a reading using a pendulum. It's somewhat limited, but great for what it does, which is giving clear answers to questions that can be answered "yes" or "no".

Where do you get a pendulum?

- You can make one. Hang a weight (fishing lure, needle, stone with a hole, key, etc) from something long and flexible (thread, cord, chain, ribbon, etc).
- You can use something you've already got, like a ring, necklace, or an i.d. on a lanyard. It's better to use something that means something to you.
- You can buy one. Rock shops, new age fairs and metaphysical stores are all good places to look for pendula.

To work with a pendulum, you first need to figure out what means "yes" and what means "no" (This can vary for different folks and different pendulums.)

- Start by holding it so it can swing freely.
- Say or think "Show me yes, please."
- Watch how it moves. Side to side? Up and down? Round and round? This is your yes for this pendulum.

- Now say or think "Show me no, please." Give it a minute and watch how the movement changes. This is your no.
- Say "Stop, please." and watch it come to a stop. Sometimes the pendulum swings so hard that you need to stop between questions to get clear answers.

Now you have "yes", "no" and "stop". The one other thing you need to know is that sometimes your pendulum will act oddly- go back and forth from yes to no, do odd movements or just stop dead. This usually means that you've asked a question that can't be answered with a simple "yes" or "no". When this happens, you may need to re-phrase the question.

For instance, what if I ask "Is the job offer I've just gotten good for me?" If the job would make me lots of money but also make me crazy, the pendulum would act oddly to tell me that I need to ask this question in a different way.

Practice working with your pendulum to get used to how it works. Start by practicing with questions you know the answers to, then ones that you don't but can easily check, in order to get confident with the process and better at asking good questions. Then, once you're ready, you can start asking questions you don't know the answers to that aren't as simple to check.

There's lots more to working with pendulums, but this gives you the basics to get started with. Try it. You'll be surprised at how much information a pendulum can give you.

Chapter 17
Applied Kinesiology

In the last chapter, we talked about using a pendulum to answer simple "yes/no" questions. Now let's talk about how to do the same thing using nothing but your intuition and your own body.

Applied Kinesiology is a system that lets you access your inner wisdom and intuition by muscle testing. It was originally developed for use with health issues, but I've found it really handy for answering questions, gaining insight and a host of other uses.

One simple process is to use your standing balance to get answers to questions that can be answered yes or no.

Start by standing with your feet tightly together and touching. For safety, stand away from other objects. Close your eyes. Think "Show me yes, please." (just like you did with your pendulum.) You'll find your body will start to either lean forward or settle back. This is your yes.

Open your eyes and re-center yourself. Close your eyes again and think "Show me no, please." You'll find your body leaning in the opposite direction for no.

Now that you've got your yes and no, it's time to practice, just like you did with the pendulum. Start with questions you already know the answers to, then ones you don't but can check easily, then ones that take a bit more checking. This is to get you used to the process.

Once you've practiced enough to feel comfortable, it's time to actually start using it. First, set your intention that you will get clear and useful answers to the questions you are asking. Next, focus on a question that can be answered "yes" or "no". Take your position, close your eyes, and see what your body tells you...

That's useful right there, but let me add another option. You can use this process to determine whether something would be a good choice for you by holding it and then asking about it.

- Pick up a vegetable at the grocery store, and ask "Is this pepper what my body needs right now?"
- Hold a book at a bookstore and think "Is there information in this book that will help me?"
- Hold a bottle of vitamins and ask "Will this brand be the best choice to support my health?"
- Hold a video. Ask "Will this show make me laugh?"

You can use this process to make better choices to support your health, happiness and spiritual growth and to avoid missteps and wasted effort. It's also handy because:

- You don't need any special equipment to do it.
- You don't need to carry that equipment with you.
- You can do it subtly in public, without people knowing what you're doing.
- It's flexible and generally useful; and, finally
- It's really affordable. No cost at all.

Like this technique? There's more to Applied Kinesiology than this, but this is all we have space for in this book. If you like it, I'd recommend that you go out and learn more about it.

Chapter 18
Making Your Own Cards

When people talk about doing readings with cards, they usually mean with tarot cards. These are beautifully illustrated cards that can be obtained in new age shops, bookstores, gift shops, and at various events. The most frequently referred to deck is the Rider Waite, the most popular deck in the world in the English speaking world. There are a host of other decks out there, some which are variations based on the Rider-Waite, and others that have their own stories, methods and systems.

Beautiful, yes. A ready made system for you to learn and use, yes. But you don't have to buy an expensive or even moderately priced deck of tarot cards. You have other options available to you.

You can do readings with regular playing cards. Do an online search of "doing readings with playing cards" for directions. Regular playing cards can often be found at dollar and discount stores, or you may even have a pack already in your home (but please note that it's better to have a deck dedicated exclusively to readings. Items that are touched a lot pick up energy, and you don't want someone's poker excitement bleeding over into your reading.)

You can make your own tarot deck. The meanings of the individual cards are available online. If you're a little bit artistic, you can use index cards or pieces of cardboard with stick figure drawings to get started. If you're more artistic, break out the colored pencils and make something wonderful. If you're not artistic, even just writing the name of the card on the card will work. The cards will work based on your intention and focus, regardless of the quality of the artwork involved (although beautiful and intricate pictures can give cues to your subconscious of the information being given.)

My husband's first working tarot deck was handmade. While not pretty, those 3 x 5 index cards with stick figures on them gave perfectly good readings, and it was only later that he replaced them with a more artistic version of the same deck that was professionally produced.

While we're at it, you can make your own version of non-tarot cards for doing readings. Be sure to include an assortment of different options and possibilities in your deck, both ones that are desirable and ones that are not so, in order to get accurate readings.

One of my early decks was a handmade one based on the roles of different angels. When I set my intention that I would get useful information using them, and kept my focus on that, I got surprisingly helpful results from my little pack of personal angel index cards.

The point is that, while professionally made decks are beautiful, cool and may give you good results, any kind of card, tarot or otherwise, is just a system for helping you get in touch with what lies in your head, your heart and your spirit. At that point, a handmade deck with symbols that mean something to you can be as effective, or even more so, than any deck bought in a store.

Chapter 19
Geomancy and Sortilege

In the last chapter, we talked about making your own deck of cards for divination, but cards are not the only way that you can do a reading. Consider, for the moment, the idea of devising your own divination method. I have a number of friends who've done this, and not only do it for fun, but also use it for doing professional readings for other people.

Start by gathering up an assortment of small items, preferable ones that fit neatly into your hand. Some good things to consider include assortments of children's plastic toys; rocks, beads and charms at rock shops; or things you have hanging out around the house. Remember that these things are going to be used exclusively for reading, so don't plan on multipurpose items. As you select things to use, set an intention that you find the items you need to do a good reading.

Next clear your items of any unneeded energy that they may have picked up before they became tools for doing a reading. Find something to keep them in, like a bowl, a basket or a bag (preferably cloth, for long term use.)

Now look at your little items, and decide what each one will mean in your reading. Perhaps the tiny plastic pig stands for business, since "this little pig went to market". Maybe the building brick stand for obstacles, as it looks like a wall. The coin means money, and the toy car means travel, but what does the little octopus say to you? If you find items in your collection that don't speak to you, trust your intuition about whether to remove them from the group or to keep them in. (They may have a meaning not currently evident to you.)

There are two ways of doing a reading with a collection like this-

- Sortilege- which is drawing items from a container, Or

- Geomancy- which is casting the items you draw and looking not only at the items but also at the ways that they fall and interact with each other.

In either case, you first set your intention that you are going to get an answer to a question of area of concern. You then focus on that question. Last, you reach into your container, and either draw out one or more items, or draw and gently cast them onto a flat surface.

When casting, items closer to you are things either coming sooner or having a more powerful effect on you, and more distant items are less of an influence or further in the future. Thinking of your question, look at what you've pulled and see what it has to tell you.

As an example, if you're wondering about love, the pig might say that you will meet someone in the process of working, whereas the brick between you and the truck can mean that there are obstacles to your love life at the present, but a change of scenery might help to open up romantic horizons.

Some people create a cloth or a board to cast items on, with markings for different areas of life. At that point, the coin that falls in the business area has a different meaning than one in the area for health.

If you use this method on an ongoing basis, you may find that items both come into and leave your collection. That's fine- these are your symbols, and what's important is what speaks to you.

Both sortilege and geomancy are systems of divination that go back through the history of mankind. If you use such a system, you've got a method that's effective and has a long history. You also have a system that is beautifully unique to you- and that may be the best system possible.

Chapter 20
Build Your Own Magickal Tools

In chapters 18 and 19, we talked about making your own cards and other tools for divination. In this chapter, let's talk about making other metaphysical tools and gadgets.

Why make your own tools?

- When you make your own tools, you can use intention and focus during creation to fill them with energy, give them a purpose, make them better at what they do and bind them to you as your own personal items to work with.
- Because you make them, you can make individual choices about things such as color, materials and appearance that particularly connect with your own energy, purpose and personal tastes.
- Tradition holds that tools you make yourself have more power.
- It's often more affordable. (You knew we'd get back here eventually, right?)
- Plus, it feels good to make a metaphysical tool, and, once it's done to your satisfaction, every time you look at it, you'll feel good again.

Don't get me wrong- I'm not saying that you can't find joy and satisfaction in tools that you buy, or that they don't work perfectly well. It's just that there's a special kind of feeling with working with something that you remember starting out as just a pile of materials on your desk.

We've looked at cards and collections of items for geomancy or sortilege. For other forms of homemade divination:

- A pendulum can be put together from any weight you find around the house suspended from a thread, string, ribbon or chain.
- A scrying mirror can be created from any decent reflective surface.
- The runes were originally written on sticks cut from a single tree. If you're collecting twigs to make a set of rune sticks, you should ask permission of the tree and thank it afterward   Birch or fruit trees are good when you're starting out. Peel the bark, and let the sticks dry before marking them with the runes. These sticks were cast (another type of geomancy) and you read the sticks themselves, and also read the patterns of runes that the sticks created together as they fell.

There's lots of ways to make your own divination systems. As two examples, my husband at one point disassembled a few inexpensive bracelets to get a collection of bone tiles which he burned with a wood burning pen for a sortilege system. I found a translation of the I Ching that I liked and hand calligraphed a copy on parchment paper which I housed in a pocket planner cover.

As to other metaphysical tools you can make yourself:

- Have a favorite crystal and want to keep it with you? Learn how to wire wrap crystals, and make your own metaphysical jewelry.
- A wand is a tool for focusing energy. You can buy an expensive hand carved one, or you can find a stick that speaks to you on a walk in the woods (Carefully dry it and strip off the bark.) You can also make a wand from crystals, copper plumbing findings and silk cord for insulation and to make it pretty.
- You can buy candles- or you can dip your own in some re-enactment museums and candle factories. You can also pour candles.
- Flower essences are powerful tools for affecting the energy around you. And they're not that hard to make. Instructions are available online.
- Permanent wards that can be used to keep bad energy out of your space can be made by securing double terminated quartz crystals in a base, such as those little wooden candle cups you find in craft stores.

Sometimes, you'll want to make things because it saves you money. Sometimes you'll want to make things because it means that you know what went into the tool, or it minimizes the energy from other people, or because it builds a stronger connection between you and your item. And sometimes you're going to want to buy things because it saves you time or energy that you need for doing other things. Either way, it's good. Trust your own inner wisdom on what's right for you.

And, if you're thinking of making something, the point is to look around you and to think outside of the box.

It's like a really cool puzzle. Got a metaphysical need? Decide what you need to accomplish, and then think about whether you already have skills or supplies that might work for that (and if not, how could you get them?)

You may be surprised at how talented you are as a crafter of metaphysical tools.

Keep in mind that, whether you buy a tool or you make your own, a metaphysical process or tool is just a method of helping you get in touch with your own inner wisdom. It's your intention that determines what that tool can do and it's your focus that fuels that process of using it. At that point, a tool made with your own hands to your own unique needs can be a powerful help in working with the energy of the world around you.

Chapter 21
Home Brewed Potions

We've talked about making your own methods of divination and other tools for energy work. Let's talk about another group of things that you can make for yourself. Let's talk about potions.

When people think about potions, they tend to think about enormous cauldrons bubbling fiercely or something involving pyrotechnics and eye of newt. The truth is that a potion is basically a liquid, drink or draft, especially one with medicinal or magick properties. (So, strictly speaking, a vitamin rich smoothie is a kind of potion.)

When mixing potions, remember to set an intention for what you are trying to accomplish, and keep your focus on your intention.

First, let's look at equipment for making potions. In a pinch, you could use your kitchen bowls and utensils for mixing up potions, but it's really better to have one set of equipment for cooking and a different set for potion making.

How come? For several reasons:

- Some ingredients in potions are edible, but some are not; and you want to keep the non-edible ones away from any food or food prep equipment.
- When reusing containers previously used for another purpose, you run the risk of physical or energetic cross-contamination. (Think of how

spaghetti sauce works its way into the fabric of a plastic container.)

- Having a separate set of equipment sends a message to your unconscious mind that you're now going to be working metaphysically, which makes it easier to set and hold an intent.

What kind of equipment do you need?

My husband, Starwolf, who does a lot more work with potions than I do, recommends the following:

- Non- reactive pots (stainless steel or teflon lined), 2 & 5 quart.
- Strainer.
- Measuring cups- 1/4-1 cup, pint and quart; plastic.
- Measuring spoons.
- Funnel.
- Ladle.
- Non-wooden stirring spoon. Wood looks good, but steel or plastic avoids cross contamination.
- Heat source, such as a hot plate.
- Storage jars and bottles.
- Mortar and pestle.

I'd add in some spray bottles, like the kind you use to put cleaning solutions in. You can start with only part of this equipment, but the above list gives you the basics you need for most potion work, and most of it can be picked up in discount stores.

One useful potion you can make for yourself is war water, an all purpose solution for dispelling negative energies and for house purification.

Put 3, 5 or 7 cut iron nails in a bottle and fill it with water. Let it sit until the nails rust. (The cloudier and nastier the water gets, the better it works.)

To use, spray or sprinkle around the person, item or place whose energy needs clearing. Traditionally iron is a protection against negative energies and entities. War water makes iron convenient to use for clearing and protection.

Another potion used to remove negative influences is four thieves vinegar.

To make it you need garlic, rosemary, rue, lavender flowers and vinegar. Put these all together in a jug or bottle and let them sit for at least ten days.

Every day, shake the bottle and say

"Evil may come,
But it will not stay.
My four thieves vinegar
Will drive evil away."

Use as a spray or floor wash to clear negative energy.

The above potions use elements that will energetically clear negative energy out and keep it from coming back, but there are a lot of different options when it comes to potions. You can use ingredients such as crystals or herbs that promote focus, ease stress or support healing if you choose.

Just remember to set your intention and keep your focus on it while you work, choose ingredients that energetically support your intention, and have tools and utensils specifically for the making of potions.

See what you can brew up.

Chapter 22
Magick and the Home

We've looked at meditation, at divination, at making your own tools and brewing your own potions. Now, let's look at how to make household tasks and recycling magickal as well. There's magick in a green lifestyle and in cleaning house!

In metaphysics, the Law of Association says that when you have two things with elements in common, what you do to one can affect the other. One perfect example of this is your home. When you make a place your home, whether you own or rent it, you develop an energetic connection with it that has metaphysical potential. The connection between your home and the folks who live there can be useful in energy work.

When working with the energy connection between you and your home, here are the basic things you need to know to start with.

- Clutter can block the energy of a space and how it flows. When things "pile up", have you noticed how that space starts to feels stale, stagnant and dead? How about how you begin to feel energized again when you clear things out and put things away?
  Part of that's psychological, but, in part, that's how physical clutter interacts with a space's energy. Some disorder can be workable, but too much clutter, especially long-term clutter, can affect the energy.

- Blocked energy can be negative, stagnant or draining. When energy's blocked and not moving freely, it becomes stale and stagnant. People in that space can feel tired, uninspired or depressed. Long term, it can even affect your personal energy and health.
- Many times, a buildup of clutter can also be symbolic of areas needing attention in our lives.
- At any time, clearing clutter can improve a space's energy, and your life as well.

The good news about this?

- You don't have to be perfect. (Thank heavens.)
- It's never too late to improve the energy of your space. Even if the closet's full of old mementos of your grade school days, sitting down now and weeding out things you don't want any more can improve your space's energy.
- You don't have to do everything. Even starting with a drawer, a bookshelf or a corner of the room can make a difference.

There's lots of ways to work with your home to improve your energy, but, for now, we're just looking at three – cleaning with intention, Feng Shui and recycling.

How do you set an intention when you clean?
Begin just before starting housecleaning, whether doing dishes, de-cluttering, or cleaning the bathroom sink. Think or say something like "Out with the old and in with

the new." Where possible, try to match the task with what you're trying to achieve. For instance:

- "As I clear out this drawer, I also clear out the patterns that kept me stuck in dead end jobs and I open my life to better jobs that fulfill me."
- "As I wash gunk off of these dishes, I also wash gunk out of my beliefs, clearing the way for more positive beliefs and a more positive reality."
- "As I get rid of old clothes that no longer fit, I also clear out old relationships that don't fit and open my life to a loving and caring partner."

Include words saying you're letting go of things that no longer serve you and bringing in things you'll be happier with to head towards what you really want.

As you wash those dishes, or clean that closet, or mop that floor, think about cleaning, but you also want to focus on your intention, so you send the energy generated by cleaning to that goal. As the act of cleaning changes what's being cleaned, make a mental and energetic link between that change and the change you want in your world. This focus helps to slant reality towards that change coming into reality.

When you finish cleaning, sit back and take a good look at what you've accomplished physically. Feel gratitude for the other good things that will soon also be present in your life.

That's it. That's really all you need to do. And you even got the dishes clean in the process...

There's another way to make housekeeping metaphysical. Feng Shui is the Chinese "way of wind and water". At its heart, it is the art of arranging objects, buildings and space to achieve energy, harmony and balance. Chinese philosophy says everything is made up of energy or "chi". When the flow of energy is free and unfettered, everything goes well and we have prosperity, health and happiness in our lives. When the flow is somehow blocked, this leads to undesirable experiences such as illness, poverty and loss.

To restore a good life, we need to do things that let blocked chi flow freely once again. In the body, we use accupressure or acupuncture to clear blocked points on the energy meridians. In the environment, we adjust the placement of furniture and other items, or use Feng Shui "cures" to compensate for items that cause blockages that cannot be moved or otherwise realigned.

There's a lot more to Feng Shui than we can cover here, so what we'll be looking at in this chapter is the Feng Shui of de-cluttering. At its simplest, Feng Shui holds that different areas of your rooms and of your house overall stand for different parts of your life. Therefore:

- When dust, clutter or broken items pile up in these areas, they negatively affect the chi of what that area stands for.
- If certain areas tend to accumulate clutter, even when you're trying to fix this, there are ongoing problems in what that area symbolizes.
- And when you clean and de-clutter those areas, the thing that area stands for tends to improve as well.

Given what we know about metaphysics, that makes perfect sense. At that point, if we want an improvement in an area of our lives, we need to:

- Know what we want to improve;
- Know the part of our homes that stands for that thing;
- Look at that area in each room (especially bedroom and office) for clutter, dust and things that are broken;
- De-clutter, clean, fix or replace these things (to improve the energy); and
- Watch things get better in our lives as the energy flows freely once more.

How do you figure that out? Picture each room divided into nine segments, like a giant tic-tac-toe board. The main entry to the room, door or arch, is always in one of the bottom three squares.

Got it? Good. Here's what the nine squares stand for.

- Top left is abundance, wealth and prosperity.
- Top middle is status, reputation and social standing.
- Top right is loving relationships.
- Middle left is roots, ancestors and family.
- The center is health and well-being.
- Middle right is creativity and offspring.
- Bottom left is deep wisdom, contemplation, and education.

- Bottom middle stands for your life path and career.
- Bottom right is mentors, guardian angels and spirits, and helpful people.

This grid applies both to individual rooms, and the house overall, so look at both spaces. Remember, you enter a space through one of the three bottom squares (Wisdom, Career or Helpful People) so stand in your doorway and line the grid up from there. When looking at specific rooms, the most important ones are the bedroom and the place in your home where you work (Home office? Where you pay the bills? The desk I'm currently writing at?) Look at those places first.

Now that you know what the spaces mean, what do you do? Pick a part of your life that you'd like to improve, and then figure out what areas in that Feng Shui grid might affect this. For instance, for progress at your job, you'll want bottom center (Career) and you might also want to look at top center (Reputation), middle right (Creativity), lower right (Helpful People), or top left (Wealth and Abundance).

Looking at these areas in your house, do you see clutter? Dust? Broken things? Dead plants? Clean, de-clutter, fix or replace things as needed, until the areas are in good, or at least better shape. As you're putting things to rights, focus on the intention that, as you straighten things up, you're improving the energy in the space and in the parts of your life the spaces stand for. That the better energy will attract better things into that area of your life.

When you're done, sit back and enjoy the results, both of a cleaner house and of better energy that brings better things into your life.

Keep an eye out for spaces that "draw" clutter. This may just be a convenient place to drop things, but it can also be a symptom of a bigger trouble spot in your life you may need to address.

Recycling is one more thing you can think about when combining housekeeping with metaphysics. Whether you're weeding out old clothes that don't fit anymore, cleaning out the basement or getting cans and bottles ready to go to the recycling center, you can always combine focus and intent with those cleaning tasks that you need to do anyway.

- Set an intention that, as you clean out items you don't need any more, you clear out stale energy and make room for better things to come in.
- Donate items to a charity and set the intention that the good energy you give to others comes back to you multiplied a hundred fold.
- Compost vegetable parings and intend that as your plants are nurtured, you'll also be nurtured.
- Brown grocery bag paper is used in quite a number of spells, particularly when something needs to be written down and discarded. Every now and then, pack your groceries in paper and reuse the bags.

Let recycling of items also be recycling of energy.

By paying attention to the energy in your space, and

using cleaning, clearing and recycling to improve it, you'll improve your own energy field as well- and it's all free and things you were going to do anyway.

Way to go, you metaphysical multi-tasker!

Chapter 23
Looking at Crystals

In metaphysics, crystals are minerals that contain vibrations. They're like metaphysical batteries for shaping the nature of reality, and the energy of a crystal can have an effect on the energy of the people, places and other things around it.

Different crystals have different vibrations. One type may be good to support emotional healing, another to give you energy to work with and a third to help you find your own inner strength. Within each type of crystals, there may be one particular stone in a bin full of them that's best for what you're trying to do. When selecting a crystal, set your intent for what you want to do with that stone and then touch the different crystals available. Many times, the right stone will feel different in a good way- which is the sign that this is the crystal you want.

Once you get a crystal home, you should clear it of any miscellaneous energy it may have picked up while being on display in the place you got it. Ways to do this include holding it under running water or letting it sit in sunlight for awhile, setting the intention that it is being cleared of all negative energy.

Some things to know to keep buying and working with crystals affordable:

- Bigger is not always better. Short of building a seat in an enormous geode or covering the walls of your home with crystals, a small crystal can do just as good of a job as a big one (and may be more affordable.)

- Perfection's overrated. While some folks rave over perfectly clear or symmetrical gem quality crystals, the truth is that an irregular crystal or one with inclusions may be fine for what you're doing.

- Some folks believe that broken crystals that have been blasted out of the ground have disrupted energy and are no good to work with. Once again, that depends on your needs and the specific crystal itself. One of my favorite crystals is an irregularly shaped chunk of rose quartz that was obviously torn from the earth but is still one of the kindest, most comforting pieces of stone I've ever found.

- Know your crystals. Find a good book with pictures or an experienced friend who will help you figure out what type of stone you want, and which type is most affordable for the task.

- Many times, there's more than one type of stone that's good for a specific task, such as healing, emotional strength, or joy. Know your options and choose the affordable one as opposed to the high priced version.

- Know your local rock shops. If you have more than one source in your area, know whose prices are best, who's most knowledgeable, and who's most helpful. Build a relationship with the shops you like the most-they'll help you find the things you want and alert you to good opportunities.

- Rock shops are also great places to get things like pendula and jewelry findings, if you want to wear your crystal.

- Many science centers and rock shops will sell

crystals of the world kits or children's grab bags. If you know your crystals, this is an affordable way to get an assortment of crystals at a very affordable price.

- Watch for rock fairs. Local and regional geological groups often stage annual rock fairs, and good deals can often be found at these.
- Buy in bulk. Crystals, especially more affordable ones, may be sold at fairs or other events in bulk bags, and be cheaper by the crystal this way. More crystals than you want? See if you can get some metaphysical friends to come in with you on this and split the bag.
- Some places around the country offer the chance to mine your own crystals at an hourly or daily fee. Search online to see if there's a mine like this near you.

There are lots of different ways to use crystals. You can wear or carry them with you to support your own energy, health or goals. You can place them around your home to improve its' energy or ward against negative energy or incursions. You can use them for making tools or potions.

It all starts with finding the crystals that are right for you. And the most important part of that is knowing what you want, and trusting your own instincts and intuition on what crystals are coming home with you.

Chapter 24
Gifts from Nature

Nature and natural practices are a traditional part of many parts of metaphysics. Whether it's herbs or stones or plants, Nature has always had a lot to offer the person who works with energy, and still does right up to today.

Nature is not one big discount store, where you can charge in and help yourself to whatever you want, but for folks who treat Her with respect, Nature has a lot to give.

Remember when you are gathering help from Nature to mind your manners and be polite. First, don't help yourself to things that belong to others. Don't pick some else's apples or clear out someone else's herb garden because you want something. Ask permission and know that the answer is sometimes "No."

Next, if you are taking cuttings from trees or plucking plants, always ask permission of the tree first and listen to your inner wisdom to hear whether it feels right to proceed (and right does not just mean that you want to.) If you take something from Nature, always express gratitude for what you have received as well.

Finally, remember to leave the area as nice as you found it. Don't randomly break off branches or litter. Nature is nicer to people who are nice to her.

Let's talk wands. A wand can be a beautiful, hand carved collectable that you acquired with great trouble and expense. A wand can also be a special stick that caught your eye in Nature.

At its simplest, a wand is just a tool and a symbol, a linear tool that helps you to mentally focus energy in a particular direction. At that point, you can perform that function with a wand you've bought, a special stick or even by pointing your finger.

If you want a wand from Nature, keep an eye out for a stick that "speaks to you" when you're out and about. Peel the bark off carefully, and leave it where you found it. Let the stick dry before you use it. After that, try working with your wand.

How does it feel in your hand? Does it help you with moving energy?

There are many uses for herbs in metaphysics, whether for smudging, potions, salves or other things. You can buy herbs, but you can also grow your own, in a garden plot, window box or small portable green house.

Growing your own means that you can keep them clean of pesticides. You can also set an intention that they are good at what you want them to do.

While we're talking about growing things, you can also turn your yard into a magickal garden. Certain plants, such as oak, rowan, thorn and ash have magickal purposes. Certain other plants provide food and shelter for birds and small animals, increasing Nature's presence in your space.

Crystals are cool, but everyday rocks can also have their own special energy or abilities. Some have special shapes that may hint at their nature. Holey stones (ones with holes worn through them) are believed to be protective, healing and helpful with psychic ability.

Watch for stones that catch your attention as you're walking.

That's only a brief look at the role of Nature in magick. There's a lot more ways that Nature can help you to work with energy, and the best ways come when you spend time with Her and listen.

Chapter 25
Spells for Pennies

When folks think about magick, one thing that often pops up is the classic magick spell. A spell is a set of words, spoken, unspoken or written, intended to invoke a magickal effect. At its simplest, a spell is just a formal way of using words for working with energy to change the nature of reality around you.

There are many traditional spells that go far back in history. There are many that were more recently developed that also work well. And you can always create a spell of your own, to suit a particular purpose or situation.

Let's take a closer look at spells.

What are the parts of a spell?

Start out with the essential pieces- our two old friends, intent (what you want to do) and focus (keeping your eye on the prize). Because it's a spell, by definition you'll need words, whether spoken, thought or written, to move the energy into movement.

Since it's a spell, words are an essential part- but what kind of words? You can use a direct statement, but many people find that words carry more energy when expressed in a rhyme.

After that, you can add optional things. Do you want to use a physical item (herb, crystal, picture, etc.) as part of the process? Physical items can be symbolic or they can carry energy that contributes to the spell itself.

Now you've got the basic pieces of a spell. Let's look at some examples…

Got someone in your life that's giving you a hard time, and want them to stop? Then try the ethically neutral "Freeze out" spell.

Either get a piece of paper with their signature on it, or write their name on a piece of brown grocery bag paper. Put it in a small waterproof container (a recycled pill bottle works well) and add enough water to cover the paper.

Close the bottle and open your freezer. Set the intention that this person will leave you alone, and say "Stay there and freeze, as long as I please." Put the bottle in the freezer, preferably tucked away behind things, and forget about it.

In most cases, you'll find that the person stops harassing you. This spell doesn't interfere with their free will- it just takes you off the general target list.

One of the major themes for spells is money and prosperity. When we're looking at money spells, green is a good color to use, and green stones such as aventurine, jade or bloodstone attract prosperity.

Take one of the above stones and clear it under running water with the intention that any negative energy will be cleared away. Hold it in your hand and set an intention that it will help you to attract more money into your life. Focus your intention on the stone and say or think nine times.

Money is coming
Easily
Welcome money
Come to me.

Keep the stone in your wallet or a piggy bank to attract more money to you.

Sometimes the old spells are the best ones. The Abracadabra spell goes back to early in recorded history, and is intended to make fevers, and other illnesses dwindle until they vanish.

Take a piece of paper, preferably parchment. Write on it as follows:

ABRACADABRA
ABRACADABR
ABRACADAB
ABRACADA
ABRACAD
ABRACA
ABRAC
ABRA
ABR
AB
A

Wear it as a necklace or armlet

(and yes, that is the same word as the one that stage magicians use today to "make things vanish". Art imitating life...)

Got a bad habit or dysfunctional belief that you want to release but you just can't seem to manage it? Got a negative situation that happens over and over in your life no matter what you do?

Write down what you want to move out of your life on a small piece of brown grocery bag paper. Take a spool of thread of any size, and tie one end firmly around your piece of paper. Set your intention to release this habit, belief or situation, and move it out of your life in an ethical manner.

Then take a walk.

As you walk, start wrapping the thread around your little piece of paper. While you do this, repeat "I bind you, I banish you, I bind you, I banish you…." to yourself.

When you wrap the last bit of the thread around the paper, say "I throw you away!" Toss the entire bundle away over your left shoulder, and then go home by a different route.

There's a lot of power in children's games…

Do you feel like someone is sending negative energy your way? This can happen when someone is jealous, spiteful or just in a bad mood. It may be aimed specifically at you, or you may just be in the wrong place at the wrong time.

If you've got someone who's messing with your vibrations, the simplest thing is just to limit your contact with them- but sometimes that's not possible. At that point, we can fall back to the "rubber-glue" method. Think or say "I'm rubber and you're glue- whatever you send bounces off me and returns to you." and set the intention that any negative energy that comes your way goes back where it came from without affecting you. If you prefer, you can also match your intent with a chorus of "Return to Sender".

This is kind of like metaphysical martial arts- using their own energy to deflect them. It's ethical because it only returns what was sent, so if they don't send negative energy, they won't get it back.

Occasionally, if the energy is specifically directed at you, the person may become more and more angry when their negative energy returns to them. For folks like that, the freeze out spell is a better choice.

Whether its ancient spells or modern rhythms, nursery rhymes or pop tunes, words combined with focus and intention are a powerful way of working with energy – and the cost of a spell depends only on the cost of any items you choose to make a part of it.

There are lots of books with standardized spells out there, both traditional and modern, but do remember that you can also start with an intention, identify the colors, elements, herbs or crystals that match that goal and create your own spell that is a custom fit for your situation. Just remember to work in keeping with ethics and respect for the free will of others, and you will be surprised at the results that you get.

Chapter 26
Alternative Health Practices

We've already talked about two free practices (meditation and visualization) that have an important place in alternative healing. Let's talk about some other inexpensive or free alternative health options.

Acupressure is a variation of the Chinese practice of acupuncture- the biggest difference being that no needles are used. Chinese medicine holds that we are all made up of energy or "chi" that flows through the body along paths known as "meridians", and that, when the meridians are clogged or blocked, illness or injury result. Acupressure lets chi flow freely by pressing on specific points on the meridians to unblock them.

I've found accupressure to be very effective for me. It's quick and easy to do, has few side effects, and the basics are easy to learn.

There's more than one way to use energy tapping for your health and well being.

Got stress, fears or phobias? Got dysfunctional beliefs that you want to get rid of but can't seem to release? Then look up Emotional Freedom Technique (E.F.T.).

E.F.T. is a method that combines affirmations (see chapter 12 Working With Sound) with tapping on certain points along the energy meridians to help you let go of beliefs, fears and phobias that are hard to release. It's easy to learn, and quick and kinda fun to do, and it works well. I've had a lot of success using E.F.T. to get rid of those dysfunctional beliefs and feelings that you know are no good but seem to be stuck in your psyche.

Interested in E.F.T? Do an online search. There are plenty of free resources to get you started with this handy technique online.

Homeopathy has been an active alternative health practice since 1790. It's based on the concept that "Like cures like" and utilizes pills containing tiny amounts of a substance to counteract the effects of a similar element. It has no side effects. I've found them helpful for such things as sprains, nausea, allergies, and general recovery.

When taking homeopathics, it's important to remember not to have anything containing camphor, caffeine, garlic, or chocolate twenty minutes before or after taking these pills. These elements interfere with the working of the homeopathics.

You can find tubes of homeopathic remedies, together with references for their use in most good health food stores.

We've been talking a lot about alternative health practices that you can learn to do for yourself or others. One other thing to look at is ways that you can receive alternative health practices from others free or affordably.

You've gotten yourself on newsletters and e-letters for things that you're interested in, right? Make sure to keep an eye on them and on local metaphysical and alternative health magazines.

- Sometimes, people will offer free or affordable introduction classes on an alternative health practice. By keeping my eyes peeled, I've spotted free Reiki 1 and accupressure classes.

- Also watch for opportunities as part of bigger events. I'm currently teaching at a convention where one teacher offers free Reiki II and Master's classes once you've paid the affordable registration for the convention. This is a great deal for a wonderful modality.
- Watch for Reiki shares or healing shares, where energy workers gather to exchange energy work. These are usually either free or ask for a donation to cover the space rental.
- Sometimes, teachers will need people willing to receive free alternative energy work from students as part of teaching that class. You may have to attend part of the class, or they may be able to do it long distance, dependant on the technique.
- And, just as there are prayer chains, there are also healing chains, where people put in requests for energywork and other people contribute.

It's good to take care of yourself, but sometimes it's also nice to have someone else take care of you.

In my life, I like to see a balance of mainstream medicine and alternative medicine. They both have wonderful things they can do to support my health, and each has pluses and minuses to consider, dependant on the situation I'm dealing with.

It's also good to know that there are some alternative medicine practices that are affordable- free or inexpensive so that they are accessible to all.

Chapter 27
Shopping Outside the Box

There are plenty of metaphysical things that you must get from someone who specifically creates them. There are lots of magickal things you need to specifically obtain through a metaphysical source, whether material or online. There are tons of things that you cannot find anyplace else besides sources targeted specifically to the metaphysical community.

But there are also quite a number of metaphysical tools, supplies and sources of information that can be found in unlikely and non- magickal places.

Magick is like that. You never know just where it's going to turn up.

So when you're looking to find the magickal things you need to follow your own path, sometimes, just sometimes, it's good to shop outside of the box...

Clearing and Protection

Salt is one of the most basic materials used in metaphysics. It can be used to absorb negative energy-sprinkle around a stale or cranky area, and then sweep up the salt with intention, carrying the negative energy away with the salt. You can clear items by burying them in salt, or letting them soak in salt water. Use a circle of salt to keep out negative influences. Salt can be found in grocery stores, dollar stores and in that shaker on your table, amongst other places.

Herbs are used throughout magick for things such

as clearing, protection and invocation. Herbs can be found in the grocery, in dollar or remainder stores, and in bulk at health food stores.

Beginning Meditation

One of the elements that most methods of meditation have in common is the use of something as a focus point. One of the better options is a candle. You can find candles in dollar and discount stores, groceries stores, and probably somewhere in your home.

While meditating, the use of "white noise", such as nature sounds or new age music, can help you to screen out distractions and find your focus. Relaxation tapes often turn up in discount stores, and relaxation recordings can also be found for free online.

The Power of Prayer

Equipment is an optional thing for prayer. Many people like to burn candles while praying. Some other things you might find helpful are religious pictures or figures, such as angels. You can often find these in dollar or discount stores.

Working With Sound

Sound has multiple applications throughout metaphysics, and there are lots of sources for inexpensive sources of sound.

Drumming can be used for meditation, ceremonial

work or to shift or clear energy. A real drum is preferable, but in a pinch, you can drum on any flat surface (I once saw a frame drumming class where the teacher supplied unused pizza boxes as practice drums for people who didn't already have one. It worked great.) You can also find drums in the kids section of discount houses.

Immediately after the holidays is a great time to shop for metaphysical sound tools. Find bells after Christmas, and pick up hollow plastic eggs after Easter to fill with gravel or other small items to make rattles.

Wind chimes are another great tool, both for white noise when meditating, and for ongoing space clearing, especially when used with Feng Shui. You'll often find small wind chimes in dollar or discount stores. Listen to them before buying to hear if their sound is a good match for your vibrations.

One inexpensive alternative to a singing bowl can be running a damp finger around the rim of a wine glass. Some glasses sing and some don't, and price doesn't seem to have any bearing on this, so you'll have to check out what you have in your collection of drinking glasses to see if you have something that'll work.

On Divination

There are lots of bits and pieces that you can use for divination and lot of inexpensive places to find them.

Index cards for making your own cards for readings can be found in stationary stores and dollar stores, and you probably have a spare pack in the bottom drawer of your desk. Ring binders from stationary or dollar stores can be used for making your own grimoires (book of spells) or a working copy of the I Ching. Those little blank books you find in dollar stores are great for recording your dreams for dream interpretation, as are assignment notebooks. Pick up a collection of small items, such as little plastic figures, at a dollar store for doing a custom sortilege or geomancy type of reading, and draw them out of a gift bag.

Build Your Own Tools

When you're working with metaphysical practices, building your own tools can be a good thing. Tools you build yourself can be more powerful and tend to be more closely tied and customized to your own energy.

Mandalas are patterns you contemplate for energy, insight and health. Find paints, inks and other writing and drawing supplies to make mandalas and other metaphysical images in dollar and discount stores, in grocery stores and at arts and crafts stores during sales. Remember to check the children's section – there are no age limits on creativity.

Like a rune or other metaphysical symbol, and want to carry it with you? Fimo clay can be used to make talismans and amulets. It's easy to use and can be found in dollar and discount stores, and at arts and crafts shops.

In Chapter 24 Gifts from Nature, we talked about finding and using a stick as a wand. You can also use a pencil for this. Remove the eraser (rubber stops energy flow) then either use as is, or put a tiny crystal in the open metal finding and use that as the sending end. Pencils are available all over the place- you probably have one in your desk right now.

While we're talking wands, you can also make a wand from copper plumbing findings from your home repair shop and crystals. Use a short length of copper piping (wrapped with silk or cotton cord or leather thong to insulate) for the body and a copper cap at each end to hold the crystals.

A brazier is handy for burning incense, and other activities that involve fire. Keep an eye out at discount stores and jumble sales for a cast iron wok or deep pot. Very safe and multifunctional.

If you're thinking about making potions or flower essences, you won't want to use your kitchen pots and pans. Check discount stores and tag sales for pots and pans that will be designated for metaphysical tasks (so you don't mix your spell work with your quick and easy dinner) and for bottles and jars to contain what you've made.

Magick and the Home

The scent of lavender, rosemary or geraniums is used in feng shui for releasing negative or stuck energy. Lemon is an energizing scent. Watch for lavender scented cleaning supplies at your grocery or dollar store, or drop a sprig of rosemary in your regular cleaning solution. Use lemon cleaning supplies from grocery or dollar store where you need to get the energy moving.

Don't forget our good friend salt for clearing negative energy, and protecting your space.

Looking at Crystals

Crystals can certainly be found in new age stores and rock shops, but there are other places to find them, especially the more common varieties of crystals. Check the children's section at nature museums and attractions, for beginning science crystal collections, or crystal grab bags. Look in beading shops and craft stores for beads made of various types of crystals. (To get a good deal, you'll need to do some research on what crystals you want and what they look like. In these situations, the crystals are frequently not labeled.)

Spells for Pennies

Candles are something used in many areas of metaphysics. When choosing a candle, think about what you're trying to accomplish and what color of candle might support that.

White- Protection, purity, peace, truth
Green- Healing, money, prosperity, luck, fertility
Brown- Physical objects, healing for animals, homes.
Pink- Emotional love, friendship
Red- Sexual love, passion, energy, enthusiasm, courage
Yellow- Clairvoyance, divination, study, learning, the mind
Purple- Power, heavy duty healing
Blue- Healing, meditation, tranquility
Orange- Strength, authority, attraction, luck
Black- Absorption or destruction of negativity

Candles work according to your intent and focus, whether they're enormous pillars or little tiny birthday cake candles. You can find them in grocery stores, discounts and dollar stores, and probably someplace in your home.

Candleholders are also available at many discount stores. Some are more noticeably metaphysical (the pillar candles in glass containers with pictures of the saints, the taper holder shaped like an angel, or the star shaped glass candle bases, for instance) but a plain candle cup or tea light holder can also be appropriate and affordable as well.

Depending on the kinds of spells you are working with, there are lots of other supplies, from spools of thread to herbs to mirrors to jewelry, that you can find in a discount store.

Alternative Health Practices

The sound of a fountain is soothing and can decrease stress. It puts moisture in the air, which can help with stuffy heads in dry months, and adding crystals to the water can put the energy of the crystals in the air as well. Check drug stores and garden supply shops for inexpensive home fountains, or buy a pump kit and make your own from things you have around the house.

Recordings of natural environments or relaxation sounds can also help you to manage stress and relax, which is good for your immune system. These recordings often turn up at discount stores and some can be found for free online.

Grocery stores, dollar stores, home repair chains, discount and remainder shops, garden shops and the drawers and closets of your own home. There are lots of good places to shop inexpensively for the bits and pieces of metaphysical work – and that's not even counting rummage sales and charity shops, where you can often find some very unique and useful things.

Sometimes, you just need to shop out of the box.

And now that we've talked about sources for inexpensive supplies for magick, I'm going to do a magick trick. In the next chapter, I'm going to be talking about the parts of metaphysics, including alternative health, that are a little more expensive, and how that can still be one of the biggest savings of all.

Catch you there.

Chapter 28
When Spending More is Spending Less

Now if you've been using some of the ideas in this book as you went along, you've probably saved some money by now. That money may have gone to your overall budget for groceries and rent and utilities. It may have gone towards letting you obtain additional affordable tools and supplies.

Let me suggest a third option.

Sometimes you may want to invest in a big ticket item. Something a little more expensive. Something with a bigger initial outlay. Something that makes you stop and think about the price.

I know. That sounds totally contrary to the basic premise of this book, right? But, truth be told, sometimes the best way to save money is to spend a little more at first. For instance:

- A more durable item that will hold up longer.
- A more expensive book that gives you all the information you need at once, rather than several small ones with one useful fact apiece.
- A large pack of tea lights that will be used over several years' worth of practices.
- Splitting the cost of a bulk pack of crystals with several like minded friends.
- Admission to a pricier convention, which gives you access to a lot of teachers and classes.
- A more expensive class with practical information that you'll use repeatedly over time.

Stuff like that.

As one good example, I completed my Reiki Master's certificate on 11/10/96. The first level cost $100, and to complete the four levels of training that I needed to get through the Master's level took me most of a year and about $1000.

I know, right? Sounds like a lot of money- but Reiki is something that I've used constantly since I first learned it, both for my own health and well-being and to help other people around me as well. It's one of the best metaphysical investments I've ever made.

When you break it down, as of the beginning of 2014, that $1000 works out to an average of less than sixteen cents a day (and since I intend to both go on living and using Reiki, that average cost is going to continue to drop.)

Less than sixteen cents a day. For an energy system that I find healthy, useful, flexible, easy to work with and an important part of my life overall.

Now that's a bargain.

That doesn't mean that everyone should run out and take Reiki (although it is a great tool.) It's more saying that you should look at the long range value of an item, as well as the immediate cost and figure it in.

Saving money in small purchases is a great way to save up a nest egg so that you can save money by making a bigger purchase if you want to.

Find out what your Reiki is.

And find the best ways to make it affordable or to afford what it is.

In Conclusion

So there you go. From the basics of magick to the basics of frugality, through divination and energy work and alternate health, we've taken a whirlwind tour of the world of magick and we've found that spending time there doesn't have to be as expensive as some people think.

The trick is to know what you want, do your research so you know where and how to look for it, and to save on the things that don't matter so you have more resources for the things that do.

The trick is to know your options and to have a plan. Now it's time for you to make yours.

Make the most of your resources and have fun. Let the magick of frugality help you bring more magick into your life.

Happy shopping!

Catherine Kane

But, Wait- There's More...

There are lots of good tips and ideas for saving money on metaphysics in this book. If you choose to use only a few of them, you'll make your magickal dollars go much further; but, if you really want to get the most for your money, a little planning and organization will help a lot.

That's what this section is about. It's got forms to help you gather and organize information, plan what you need to get and reach out to the sources that best meet your needs.

- The planning list is for making lists of the supplies you need for specific projects, and alternatives if your first choice is too expensive or unavailable.
- The sources list is for looking at your options for getting the different things you want, so you can make good choices.
- The contact list is for information about your different sources, to make contacting them simple.

I've included a blank copy of each form, and an example of how it can be used. You can copy these forms and use them as they are, or use them as a jumping off spot to create your own forms to suit your unique needs.

I'd recommend that you buy a ring binder (preferably on sale), hole punch whatever forms you choose, and keep your information together and accessible. At that point, if you start a new practice, you'll already have lots of information that can help you get started easily and affordably.

And that's a really good deal.

Metaphysical Supplies-
Planning List

Practice   **Items Needed**   **Alternatives**

Metaphysical Supplies-
Planning List (example)

Practice	Items Needed	Alternatives
Prosperity grid	Emeralds (6)	Aventurine (6)
		Jadeite (6)
Meditation	Guided Meditation Tapes	Nature recordings
		Chanting recordings
Divination	Index cards	
	Colored pencils	Crayons
	List of standard cards found online for inspiration	

Metaphysical Supplies-
Sources List

Item	Sources	Notes

Metaphysical Supplies-
Sources List (example)

Item	Sources	Notes
Crystals	Visions	Good selection, informative staff, pricey
	The Black Cat	Good selection and info, better prices
	The Rock Shop	Good selection, regular sales, not much metaphysical information
	Annual Gem/ Mineral Show	Once a year, great prices, plan ahead
Candles	Visions	Beautiful candles, pricey
	Museum village	Put in intention while you dip your own
	Dollar Store	Inexpensive, smudge to remove any energy they may have picked up
Books	Visions	New books, knowledgeable staff, more expensive
	The Black Cat	More affordable, good used book section
	Local book store	Selection small, discount card
	Used book store	Good prices, limited stock

Metaphysical Resources-
Contact List

Name	Contact Information	Notes

Metaphysical Resources-
Contact List (example)

Name	Contact Information	Notes
	Address	*prices, classes*
	Phone	*what is this a*
	Email	*source for?*
	Website	
	Hours	
	Contact person	

…and Even More Yet…

When you're talking about free and inexpensive resources in metaphysics, one great truth is that change is inevitable.

I've tried to give you a good overview of different ways to save money in metaphysics, but because change is always happening, there are lots of good references that may be around for awhile and then vanish as quickly as they came.

In order to give you the best options possible (and to not be continually updating this book), I'm therefore offering you the following reference as a bonus to this volume.

For an ongoing selection of articles on practical living in a magickal world, check out my blog at www.ForesightYourCTPsychic.wordpress.com.

And, for an assortment of helpful links, books, websites and other inexpensive or practical references, check out the Useful Resources page on my website at http://www.foresightyourpsychic.com/UsefulResources.ht ml .

No cost to you. Because, if you've bought this book, you're interested in saving money in metaphysics, and I want you to have the best options possible.

Catherine Kane

Glossary

Acupressure - Chinese way of promoting health by clearing blocked chi through pressure on points along energy meridians.

Affirmations- a positive statement, repeated to change conscious and unconscious patterns of belief and behavior.

Applied Kinesiology - way of gaining information by asking questions and then testing the strength and balance of the body.

Chanting- repeating words or sounds on a limited range of notes to clear the mind, induce a trance state or connect with spirit.

Clearing- removing negative or unwanted energy from a person, place or thing.

Divination- Gaining information by psychic methods.

Dowsing - using tools such as pendulums, forked sticks and L-rods for divination, to locate ley lines or to find things.

Emotional Freedom Technique (E.F.T.) - system combining tapping on accupressure points with affirmations to release fears, phobias and dysfunctional beliefs.

Energy - the basic element that everything in the Universe is made of.

Feng Shui - Chinese system of energywork that affects your life by changing your environment.

Focus- what your attention and energy is directed towards at any moment.

Free Will- the ability to make choices and have some control over your life through these choices.

Geomancy - divination by drawing items from a container, casting them on a surface, and looking at the items and how they interact.

Grimoire - book of spells.

Grounding- a) connecting with the earth. b) clearing out negative or unwanted energy into the earth.

Homeopathy- alternative healing technique, where small amounts of a substance help to clear problems caused by greater amounts.

I Ching- Chinese divination by the drawing and casting of coins or yarrow stalks.

Intention- the goal for a metaphysical practice.

Intuition- knowing through methods other than the five senses.

Karuna Reiki - type of Reiki that uses sound.

Law of Attraction- "Like Calls to Like"; you attract more of the kind of thing you primarily focus on.

Law of Association- when two things have elements in common, what you do to one can affect the other.

Magick - energywork to change your reality. Spelled with a "k" to distinguish it from stage "magic".

Meditation - techniques for calming the mind for health, well-being and spirituality.

Metaphysics - overall term for alternative or non-physical ways of affecting the world around you, such as magick, energywork, and alternative health practices.

"The Monkey Mind"- mental distractions or "chattering".

New Age - metaphysical category that combines practices from different cultures and times. (There has been more than one New Age.)

Omen - a prophetic sign.

Pendula - Plural of pendulum.

Pendulum - tool for dowsing using a suspended weight that swings freely. Can be used for divination.

Portent- An indication of something about to occur; omen.

Potion - a liquid, drink or draft, especially one with medicinal or magickal properties.

Reiki - Japanese energywork for health and well-being.

Reiki shares- gatherings where Reiki practitioners get together to exchange Reiki and Reiki techniques.

"Repeaters"- crystals used to keep an energy field in place for long term use.

Scrying- divination by looking in a reflective surface, such as a mirror or crystal.

Signs - signals that indicate experiences to come.

Smudging- clearing the energy of a space with smoke or sound.

Sortilege - divination by drawing items from a container.

Spell- format for working magick. Usually involves words (spoken/ thought/ written.)

Sunwards - clockwise.

Visualization - type of meditation involving mentally focusing on a goal using as many senses as possible.

Warding- protecting a space from negative or unwanted energy or visitors.

Widdershins - counter-clockwise.

Index

Who is Catherine Kane?

Catherine Kane is a writer, professional psychic, bard, Reiki master, story teller, Christian mystic, teacher, speaker, enthusiastic student of the Universe, maker of very bad puns and overachiever (amongst other things...) She is fascinated with things metaphysical, spiritual, self improvement and alternative health.

With so much territory to cover, she is also a careful manager of her resources- and a very clever shopper.

She has written five other books so far – "Adventures in Palmistry", "The Practical Empath- Surviving and Thriving as a Psychic Empath", "Manifesting Something Better", "The Psychic Power of Your Dreams" and "The Lands That Lie Between" (an urban fantasy novel.) The odds are good that she'll continue to carry on in this fashion.

Visit Catherine at
www.CatherineKaneWrites.wordpress.com
and as Catherine Kane Writes on Facebook

Catherine can also be found with her husband Starw olf
as Foresight at
www.ForesightYourPsychic.com,
www.ForesightYourCTPsychic.wordpress.com
or as Foresight on Facebook.

Also by Catherine Kane

Adventures in Palmistry

Your Destiny is in your hands – and you can have a hand in your destiny! Reading palms can empower and enlighten you, giving you the information you need for the adventure of life, and enabling you to help others around you. And it can be a lot of fun, as well. "Adventures in Palmistry" makes palmistry easy and fun. It will put the power of palmistry in your hands.

The Practical Empath- Surviving and Thriving as a Psychic Empath

Do other people say you're too sensitive? Do other people's emotions overwhelm you? Do you carry abdominal weight you can't seem to lose?

You may be a psychic empath, tuned into emotional energy which can empower or drain you. To use that gift to help yourself and others, you need to learn skills that put you in control of your gift.

This is the book to help you do just that...

The Lands That Lie Between-
An Urban Fantasy with Morgan and Sam

The day that Morgan lost her job, she knew that change was coming. She broke her lease, threw everything she valued in life, including her cat Sam, in her van, kissed her adoptive family goodbye, and started a cross country trek.

She knew change was coming. She expected that.

What she wasn't expecting was elves, or magick walking in the world around her, or the beauty and the danger of the Lands that Lie Between…

Manifesting Something Better-
Easy, Quick and Fun Ways
To Manifest the Life Of Your Dreams

We are always manifesting- so why don't we manifest something better? The world is made of energy and our own energy determines the things, people and experiences in our lives. Better energy-better life. The trick is to know how to use your energy to manifest the life you want. This book is here to tell you how to do just that. It's full of simple methods for improving your energy and working with it to manifest the things you want in your life. Easy, fun and practical. Are you manifesting something better? This book will give you the skills you need.

The Psychic Power of Your Dreams: Practical Skills for Working With Your Dreams For Insight, Information, Creativity and a Better Life

Your dreams are the doorway to your psychic self. We are all psychic- and dreams are the way most of us first get in touch with our intuition. Dreams bypass blocks and judgment, and put us in contact with our natural inner wisdom. It's easy- and this book will teach you how. You'll learn: • The types of dreams, (Which one are you having?) • How to remember your dreams, • A simple way to interpret your personal dreams, • How to dream to access your psychic ability, • How to deal with problem dreams, • And much, much more. Awaken your own psychic gifts through your dreams. This book will show you how.

For more information on these books, please visit Foresight Publications at www.ForesightYourPsychic.com

www.ingramcontent.com/pod-product-compliance
Lightning Source LLC
Chambersburg PA
CBHW030934090426
42737CB00007B/428